# PLAYING
## WITH
# PURPOSE

### BASEBALL DEVOTIONS

Interior images: Associated Press

Published by Barbour Publishing, Inc., P.O. Box 719, Uhrichsville, Ohio 44683, www.barbourbooks.com

*Our mission is to publish and distribute inspirational products offering exceptional value and biblical encouragement to the masses.*

Member of the
Evangelical Christian
Publishers Association

Printed in the United States of America.

# PLAYING
# WITH
# PURPOSE

## BASEBALL DEVOTIONS

180 Spiritual Truths Drawn
from the Great Game
of Baseball

**PAUL KENT**

SERIES EDITOR
**MIKE YORKEY**

BARBOUR
PUBLISHING

# WELCOME TO PLAYING WITH PURPOSE: BASEBALL DEVOTIONS

Is it appropriate to combine America's Pastime with God's Word? Of course!

The apostle Paul wrote the sports of his day into letters that became our scriptures. You'll find biblical lessons related to running races (1 Corinthians 9:24), wrestling (Ephesians 6:12), and even boxing (1 Corinthians 9:26). So why shouldn't we draw insights from the great game of baseball?

In the pages ahead, you'll find 180 readings that highlight some intriguing aspect of big league baseball, each coupled with a brief, thought-provoking spiritual point. Read the stories for love of the game; mull the takeaways for love of the Lord.

Since its beginning in 1876, Major League Baseball has been a mainstay of American culture—while often drawing players and fans from around the world. In *Playing with Purpose: Baseball Devotions*, you'll meet hundreds of players, both famous and unknown, and relive great moments from nearly a century and a half of competition.

Throughout that long history, many of the more than sixteen thousand major league players have been solid, upstanding Christians. Some have been foul-mouthed, hard-drinking, less-than-exemplary individuals. These devotionals generally don't judge a player's character—they simply draw life lessons from their exploits on the field.

But sprinkled through this devotional, you'll also find a profile of a current Christian ballplayer drawn from Barbour Publishing's *Playing with Purpose: Inside the Lives and Faith of Major League Stars*. That book's lead author was Mike Yorkey, who serves as editor of this devotional and provides an in-depth view of the career and spiritual journey of several major leaguers.

Speaking of the major leagues, every baseball fan knows there are two: the National League, dating to the United States' centennial year of 1876, and the American League, beginning in 1901. What many don't realize is that, during the National League's first twenty-five years, there were several *other* "major leagues"—including the American Association (1882–91, featuring teams such as the Louisville Colonels, Columbus Buckeyes, Kansas City Cowboys, and Rochester Hop Bitters), the Union Association (1884, including the Altoona Mountain City, Pittsburgh Stogies, St. Paul Apostles, and Wilmington Quick Steps), and the Players League (1890, including the Brooklyn Wards Wonders, Buffalo Bisons, Cleveland Infants, and Philadelphia Quakers). Only one major league—the Federal League (1914–15), featuring the Baltimore Terrapins, Brooklyn Tip-Tops, Buffalo Buffeds, Chicago Whales, Indianapolis Hoosiers, Kansas City Packers, Newark Peps, Pittsburgh Rebels, and St. Louis Terriers—attempted to compete with the "Big Two" in the twentieth century.

As you can tell by their dates, none of these other leagues had staying power. But they were considered "major," and you'll see them referenced occasionally throughout this book. You'll also find many references to current teams that have changed cities (for example, the Boston/Milwaukee/Atlanta Braves), names (such as the Houston Colt .45s/Astros), or both (like the St. Louis Browns/Baltimore Orioles or the Montreal Expos/Washington Nationals). You'll read about more than four hundred players, managers, executives, and others connected to the great game of baseball.

And—we hope—you'll find spiritual truths to inform, encourage, and challenge you as you live your own Christian life each day.

PAUL KENT, AUTHOR
MIKE YORKEY, EDITOR

Baseball stars come and go, but some players will be remembered as long as the game continues.

For most major leaguers, fame is fleeting. For example, what do you remember about Pat Putnam, Bob Turley, or Al McBean? *The Sporting News* called

**THE IMMORTALS**

them the 1974 American League Rookie Player of the Year, the 1964 National League Reliever of the Year, and the 1958 Major League Player of the Year, respectively. Their achievements, however important in their day, have largely been relegated to baseball's history books.

Some stars, though, have truly stood the test of time. For recording 714 home runs, 2,213 runs batted in, and a .342 lifetime batting average, Babe Ruth remains the standard by which sluggers are judged more than sixty-five years after his death. For breaking Ruth's home run record and finishing his career with 755 round trippers—an average of almost 33 home runs a season over his twenty-three years in the game—Hank Aaron achieved lasting fame. For winning 511 games in a twenty-two-year pitching career, Cy Young set an apparently unbreakable record—and lent his name to the annual award for the leagues' best hurlers. They and a few others—Ty Cobb, Jackie Robinson, and Joe DiMaggio among them—can be called baseball's "immortals."

Most of us would like to be remembered for something we've accomplished or some good we've done. But true immortality is found only in Jesus Christ. He said it Himself in one of the Bible's best-known verses: "For God so loved the world that he gave his one and only Son, that whoever believes in him shall not perish but have eternal life" (John 3:16).

Baseball immortality is cool. Real immortality, through God's gift of salvation, is priceless.

*In the way of righteousness there is life;*
*along that path there is immortality.*
PROVERBS 12:28

Baseball has a number of "exclusive clubs"—the 300 win club, the 500 home run club, and the 3,000 strikeout club, to name a few.

Years of toil typically precede such honors, but one exclusive club

**HIGH EXPECTATIONS**

welcomes players who've never appeared in a major league game. Since 1965, one person each season has become baseball's number one draft choice—the first player selected in the first round of the major league lottery.

Familiar names fill the list: Since the Kansas City A's took catcher Rick Monday in the very first player draft, pitcher Andy Benes, outfielder Harold Baines, third baseman Bob Horner, and shortstop Chipper Jones have all been No. 1 picks. So have Darryl Strawberry, Ken Griffey Jr., Alex Rodriguez, B. J. Surhoff, Floyd Bannister, Jeff King, Tim Belcher, Josh Hamilton, and Adrian Gonzalez.

Though several players parlayed their No. 1 status into solid, even spectacular, baseball careers, others have been less successful. Al Chambers, the No. 1 draft pick of 1979, played only 57 games over three seasons with Seattle, posting two career home runs and a lifetime batting average of .208.

High expectations accompany the honor of the No. 1 draft choice. In a similar way, God expects more from those of us He's blessed with particular talents, qualities, or possessions. "From everyone who has been given much, much will be demanded," Jesus said, "and from the one who has been entrusted with much, much more will be asked" (Luke 12:48).

God's gifts were never meant to be hoarded. Today, ask yourself two questions: How has God especially blessed me? How can I share that blessing with others?

*Now it is required that those who have been given a trust must prove faithful.*
1 CORINTHIANS 4:2

A memorable name wasn't the only thing Dave Philley had going for him.

Over an eighteen-year major league career, Philley played for eight different teams: the White Sox, Athletics, Indians, Orioles, Tigers, Giants, Red Sox, and—you guessed it—the Phillies, too. It was with the Phillies that Philley would set a major league record for most consecutive pinch hits.

**IN THE CLUTCH**

In 1958, his first full year in Philadelphia, Philley appeared in 91 games, tallying 207 at bats. He recorded a nifty .309 average on 64 hits, including eight straight pinch hits to end the season.

But Philley's string had yet to snap. On Opening Day of the 1959 season, he rapped still another pinch hit, establishing a record of nine in a row. Two years later, playing in Baltimore, Philley would set an American League record by smacking 24 pinch hits for the season.

In the clutch, Dave Philley was a tough out. Under the pressures of life, we as Christians can be unstoppable.

Warning His disciples of persecutions to come, Jesus also gave a promise of heavenly wisdom and power: "When you are brought before synagogues, rulers and authorities, do not worry about how you will defend yourselves or what you will say, for the Holy Spirit will teach you at that time what you should say" (Luke 12:11–12).

The same Spirit who powered Peter, James, John, and the gang lives in you today, too. Think about that next time you're needed in the clutch.

*"The Advocate, the Holy Spirit, whom the Father*
*will send in my name, will teach you all things and will*
*remind you of everything I [Jesus] have said to you."*
JOHN 14:26

When the Red Sox won the 2004 World Series, Boston fans could lay to rest some of the more painful memories of their team's failures—like its infamous 1978 collapse.

**MASSACRE**

Twenty-six years before reaching the pinnacle of baseball glory, it appeared the Sox, always the poor stepsister of the American League East, might actually make it to the ball. Boston cruised through the first half of the season, building a whopping 14½ game lead by July 19. But the stumbling Yankees, under new manager Bob Lemon, began a remarkable comeback in late July, pulling to within four games of the Sox in early September.

In the opener of a four-game series at Fenway Park, the Yankees ripped the Red Sox, 15–3. Game 2 went to the Bronx Bombers as well, 13–2. New York then swept Games 3 and 4, 7–0 and 7–4, to pull even in the race, ultimately winning the pennant in a one-game playoff when Bucky Dent launched a memorable home run off Mike Torrez.

Baseball fans dug deep into American history to find an appropriate label for the late-season disaster, coming up with the "Boston Massacre."

Massacres are terrible things, generally. But you could make a strong case for them in the spiritual realm. "If you live according to the flesh, you will die," the apostle Paul wrote to Christians in Rome, "but if by the Spirit you put to death the misdeeds of the body, you will live" (Romans 8:13–14). Lust, dishonesty, anger, unforgiveness—kill them all, Paul says.

That kind of massacre is a good thing.

*We know that our old self was crucified with him
so that the body ruled by sin might be done away
with, that we should no longer be slaves to sin.*
ROMANS 6:6

Triple plays are rare enough, but those of the unassisted variety are extraordinarily uncommon.

Throughout Major League Baseball's long history—in literally tens of thousands of games—approximately a dozen unassisted

# TRIPLE PLAY—UNASSISTED

triple plays have occurred. Interestingly, six of those happened in the 1920s, including the only instance ever in World Series competition.

The date was October 10, 1920. The place: Cleveland's League Park, where Game 5 of the best-of-nine Fall Classic was under way between the Indians and the Brooklyn Dodgers. In the fifth inning, Tribe second baseman Bill Wambsganss speared a line drive off the bat of Brooklyn pitcher Clarence Mitchell then stepped on second to double up his Dodger counterpart Pete Kilduff, who had broken toward third. When "Wamby" spun to throw toward first, he found Brooklyn catcher Otto Miller hung up near second and tagged him for the third out of the inning. It took a moment for the League Park crowd to realize just what had happened, but they soon broke into a rousing ovation for the one-man triple killing.

Though the unassisted triple play can and does occasionally occur, it's not something to be expected. Isn't it nice to know that, in the Christian life, God doesn't expect us to accomplish our tasks single-handedly, either? Whatever He's called us to do, He's also provided fellow believers who can help and encourage us—while He works in the background for everyone's benefit. As Ecclesiastes 4:12 says, "A cord of three strands is not quickly broken."

That's a "triple play" that will never be equaled.

*Carry each other's burdens, and in this*
*way you will fulfill the law of Christ.*
GALATIANS 6:2

You might have trouble finding Clifty, Arkansas, on a map. But the tiny town is known as the birthplace of Hall of Fame shortstop Joseph Floyd Vaughan.

## THE MAN FROM ARKANSAS

Vaughan entered the big leagues with Pittsburgh in 1932 at the tender age of twenty. His youth, however, was no detriment to his play—he batted .318 in 129 games that rookie season, driving in 61 runs for the second-place Pirates. For the next nine years, Vaughan batted over .300, including a league-leading .385 in 1935. He led the league three times each in runs scored, triples, and bases on balls, and between 1934 and 1942 he was chosen for nine straight All-Star teams—eight times with Pittsburgh and once with the Brooklyn Dodgers. Retiring after fourteen seasons with a .318 career batting average, Vaughan was voted into the Hall of Fame in 1985.

The statistics are impressive, but it was a nickname that makes the man truly memorable. In honor of his home state, Joseph Floyd Vaughan was generally known as "Arky."

Nearly two thousand years ago, in a city of Asia Minor, believers in Jesus took on a special name to honor their Lord: "The disciples were first called Christians at Antioch" (Acts 11:26). Meaning "followers of Christ," the name made a clear statement to the world at large, showing that these people were serious about their commitment to the teaching, the example, and the person of Jesus.

The name *Christian* should still stand for such commitment. Live your life in a way that makes the meaning of "Christian" as obvious as that of "Arky."

*Follow my example, as I follow the example of Christ.*

1 CORINTHIANS 11:1

A natural athlete, Allie Reynolds had been pursued by track, football, and basketball coaches in college.

But he chose to play baseball, breaking into the big leagues as a twenty-five-year-old rookie late in 1942. The 6-foot right-hander spent his first five years in Cleveland and won in double figures each of his first four complete seasons. His high point as an Indian was in 1945, when he went 18–12 with a 3.20 earned run average and picked up an All-Star team selection.

**SUPERCHIEF**

In 1947, after a trade to the Yankees, Reynolds really starred. He went 19–8 that year, his .704 winning percentage leading the American League. For the next five years, he never won fewer than 16 games, notching a personal best of 20 wins in 1952. With New York, Reynolds would earn five more All-Star selections.

For his thirteen-year career, Allie Reynolds won 182 games against 107 losses for a lifetime winning percentage of .630. He posted a career ERA of 3.30, striking out 1,423 batters. Part Native American, born in the former Indian Territory of Oklahoma, Allie Reynolds boasted an appropriate nickname: "Superchief."

The apostle Paul once called himself the chief, but not in pride: "This is a faithful saying and worthy of all acceptation, that Christ Jesus came into the world to save sinners, of whom I am chief" (1 Timothy 1:15 KJV). The New International Version of the Bible translates *chief* here as "the worst."

Maybe you feel like Paul today—the chief of sinners. If so, reread what comes before: "Christ Jesus came into the world to save sinners." Isn't that "worthy of all acceptation"?

*"The tax collector stood at a distance. He would not even look up to heaven, but beat his breast and said, 'God, have mercy on me, a sinner.' I tell you that this man ... went home justified before God."*
LUKE 18:13–14

How would you feel if you played nineteen seasons for the same team and never won a pennant? And what if, in most of those seasons, your team was deep in the standings—three times dead last?

**MR. (YOUR TEAM HERE)**

If you were Chicago Cubs star Ernie Banks, you'd keep playing hard—and racking up some impressive personal statistics. In your third year in the big show, 1955, you'd be the first major league shortstop to hit more than 40 home runs in a season. You'd set a major league record that same year with five grand slams. You'd lead the league in home runs—with 41— while winning a Gold Glove in 1960. You'd win back-to-back Most Valuable Player awards in 1958 and 1959—becoming the only player ever from a second-division team to do so. (Before the 1969 season, when expansion caused a realignment of both leagues and the start of postseason playoffs, teams that ranked in the bottom half of the league standings were said to be in the "second division," while teams in the top half—the top four teams in an eight-team league—were said to be in the "first division.")

But no matter how badly your team was doing, you'd arrive at the ballpark every day with a contagious love of the game. You'd be known for loving the game so much that you'd said, "Let's play two!" You'd show a happy, outgoing disposition that earns you the nickname "Mr. Cub."

If Ernie Banks could be so happy on a perpetually bad ball club, shouldn't we as Christians have even more joy in our daily lives? After all, isn't it true that God "has blessed us in the heavenly realms with every spiritual blessing in Christ" (Ephesians 1:3)?

If we're honest, we have to admit that most of the things that irritate and depress us are minor, hardly worthy of the emphasis we put on them. Keep your focus on the goodness of God and the blessings He lavishes on you—and develop a reputation as "Mr. (Your Team Here)" in your own field of endeavor.

*This is the day which the LORD hath made;*
*we will rejoice and be glad in it.*
PSALM 118:24 KJV

"Big Ed" Delahanty had it going on.

The foremost of five major league siblings (brothers Frank, Jim, Joe, and Tom also reached the big show), Ed Delahanty was one of baseball's brightest stars at the dawn of the twentieth century. With the Phillies from 1892 to 1899, Delahanty led the league in almost every offensive category: home runs (19 in 1893, 13 in '96); runs batted in (146 in 1893, 126 in '96); triples (21 in 1892), doubles (49, 44, and 55 in 1895, '96, and '99); and hits (238 in 1899). In the final season of the 1800s, Delahanty posted a league-high batting average of .410. Impressive, yes, but not even the first time Delahanty batted better than .400. He hit .404 in both 1894 and '95, though neither of those figures led the league.

**INVINCIBLE**

In the century following, no other player attained Delahanty's lifetime batting average of .346. Good for fourth place all-time, the record seems invincible—like Delahanty's hard-playing, hard-drinking baseball persona.

That illusion was shattered on July 2, 1903. A railroad conductor who said Delahanty was imbibing whiskey and causing trouble tossed the player off his train at the Canadian side of the International Bridge. When Delahanty tried to cross the span on foot, he fell into the Niagara River to his death. He was thirty-five years old.

"No one has power over the wind to contain it," said the writer of the Bible's book of Ecclesiastes, "so no one has power over the time of their death" (8:8). In this life, there's no such thing as invincibility.

That's the bad news. The good news is this: through Jesus Christ, death opens the door to a truly invincible life.

*This grace was given us in Christ Jesus before the beginning of time, but it has now been revealed through the appearing of our Savior, Christ Jesus, who has destroyed death and has brought life and immortality to light through the gospel.*
2 TIMOTHY 1:9–10

It's hard to have a better debut than John Paciorek.

A right fielder for the Houston Colt .45s (the original name of the Astros), John was the first of three Pacioreks to reach the major leagues.

**FAST START**

He played his first game in 1963, seven years before younger brother Tom began an eighteen-season career with six teams, and twenty-four years before baby brother Jim played a partial season for the Milwaukee Brewers. As rookies, Tom and Jim were following in some big footsteps.

In Houston's final game of '63, on September 29, John cracked three hits in three at bats, walked twice, drove in three runs, and scored four times in the Colt .45s' 13–4 win over the Mets. Even more remarkable than that opening night performance is the fact that John Paciorek never played another major league game. Slowed by back problems, he toiled in the minors over the next six years before retiring from baseball at age twenty-four.

Paciorek's fast start brings to mind Jesus' parable of the soils. A farmer was sowing seed, some of which "fell on rocky places, where it did not have much soil. It sprang up quickly, because the soil was shallow. But when the sun came up, the plants were scorched, and they withered because they had no root" (Matthew 13:5–6).

What did that mean? Jesus later explained, "The seed falling on rocky ground refers to someone who hears the word and at once receives it with joy. But since they have no root, they last only a short time. When trouble or persecution comes because of the word, they quickly fall away" (13:20–21).

Spiritually speaking, a fast start is no guarantee of future results. What really matters is a lifelong embrace of God's truth.

> *"The one who hears my words and does not put them into practice is like a man who built a house on the ground without a foundation. The moment the torrent struck that house, it collapsed and its destruction was complete."*
>
> LUKE 6:49

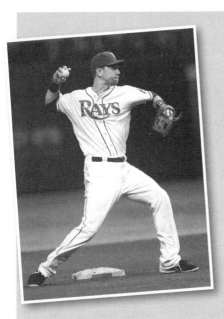

# BEN ZOBRIST

**Born:** May 26, 1981
**Height:** 6' 3"
**Weight:** 200 pounds
**Throws:** Right
**Bats:** Both

**Quote:** "To me, coming from Eureka (Illinois), where no other athlete had played anything in professional sports, was definitely huge. It was like God was saying, *Look what I can do for you if you commit your work to Me and you just follow Me where I want you to go. I can do some things that you don't think are even possible.*"

## MAJOR LEAGUE RECORD

*Drafted:* 6th round by Houston Astros, 2004

*MLB debut:* August 1, 2006 (age 25), with Tampa Bay Devil Rays

*Stat highlights:* 27 home runs, .297 batting average (2009), 91 RBIs (2009, 2011), 46 doubles (2011)

Baseball has not only weathered the nation's war efforts but also contributed to their success.

Connecting the national pastime with national security during World War II, President Franklin D. Roosevelt urged game officials to play through the conflict. In a note to baseball commissioner Kenesaw Mountain Landis (called by historians the "Green Light Letter"), Roosevelt wrote, "It would be best for the country to keep baseball going. . . . Everybody will work longer hours and harder than ever before. And that means that they ought to have a chance for recreation."

**GOOD SOLDIERS**

While many Americans went to the ballparks, many ballplayers went to war. Some of the game's greatest stars—Hank Greenberg, Bob Feller, Ted Williams, and others—interrupted their careers for World War II duty. Others served, never to return: Elmer Gedeon, who played briefly with the Washington Senators in 1939, became the first former major leaguer killed in action on the battlefields of France.

Today, though few stars enlist, baseball often honors the men and women who do. Consider the San Diego Padres, who wear special camouflage uniforms on their annual "Military Opening Day" as well as for every Sunday home game.

We recognize good soldiers for their commitment and service—and we're called to the same qualities in our faith. The apostle Paul once compared the Christian life to the military, telling his protégé Timothy, "Join with me in suffering, like a good soldier of Christ Jesus." Continuing the analogy, Paul wrote, "No one serving as a soldier gets entangled in civilian affairs—but rather tries to please his commanding officer" (2 Timothy 2:3–4).

"General Jesus" leads us today. Are you being a good soldier?

*Whatever you do, work at it with all your heart, as working for the Lord, not for human masters, since you know that you will receive an inheritance from the Lord as a reward. It is the Lord Christ you are serving.*
COLOSSIANS 3:23–24

*Exuberance:* the quality of being exuberant—joyously unrestrained and enthusiastic. What better description of Joe Carter on October 23, 1993?

You can't fault Carter for being excited. The eleven-year veteran, in his third season with the Toronto Blue Jays, had just done something never before seen in Major League Baseball: he slammed a walk-off home run to end a World Series.

**EXUBERANCE**

Carter, who hit 33 homers that season, came to bat in the bottom of the ninth against Philadelphia closer Mitch "Wild Thing" Williams. Though the Blue Jays led the series three games to two, they trailed the Phillies 6–5 in Game 6. With one out and two on, Carter ripped a 2–2 fastball over the left field fence to give Toronto its second straight World Series title—and make baseball history.

Many fans remember the thirty-three-year-old Carter's laughing, leaping, skipping home run trot, as well as the joyful mob scene at home plate where Blue Jay teammates joined in his exuberant celebration.

Did you know God is into joyous celebrations, too? In Jesus' story of the prodigal son who returns home, the boy's father—representing God Himself—tells his servants, "Quick! Bring the best robe and put it on him. Put a ring on his finger and sandals on his feet. Bring the fattened calf and kill it. Let's have a feast and celebrate" (Luke 15:22–23).

Sin happens. We all stray from God at one time or another. But our heavenly Father is thrilled anytime His children turn from sin and come back to Him. Don't ever be afraid to return home—there's an exuberant welcome awaiting you.

*" 'This son of mine was dead and is alive again;*
*he was lost and is found.' So they began to celebrate."*
LUKE 15:24

It's bad enough to go oh-fer one game—getting no hits in three or four at bats. Then there's the slump: "Here comes Smith, who's oh-fer his last eleven trips to the plate." But oh-fer an entire season?

**OH-FER**

Backup catcher Hal Finney holds the dubious distinction as the nonpitcher with the major league's worst oh-fer season, going hitless in 35 at bats in 1936. The native Alabaman, playing for the Pittsburgh Pirates, started off with promise in '31 when his eight hits in 26 at bats yielded a season average of .308. But things went downhill from there.

Finney's sophomore year with the Bucs featured seven more at bats but one fewer hit—and his average dipped to .212. It increased slightly the next season, the busiest of his career, when he slapped 31 hits in 133 at bats for an average of .233. In 1934 Finney appeared in only five games and had no official at bats.

After a year out of the majors, Finney returned to Pittsburgh in 1936 for his final tour of duty in the big leagues. His last campaign would include appearances in 21 games, 35 official at bats, and a grand total of zero base hits. Finney would be out of the majors after turning in his record-setting goose egg.

Like a player suffering an oh-fer season, every one of us falls short of God's perfection. No matter how hard we may try, we fail. As the prophet Isaiah once wrote: "All of us have become like one who is unclean, and all our righteous acts are like filthy rags; we all shrivel up like a leaf, and like the wind our sins sweep us away" (Isaiah 64:6).

It's good to know that God's grace can erase the embarrassment of our human futility.

> *[God] saved us, not because of righteous*
> *things we had done, but because of his mercy.*
> TITUS 3:5

American League MVP voters faced a challenge in 1978.

On one hand, they had Red Sox outfielder Jim Rice, who appeared in every one of Boston's 163 games, including a single-game playoff between the Beantown boys and the New York Yankees. Rice put up league-leading numbers in several categories, including hits (213), triples (15), home runs (46), runs batted in (139), and slugging average (.600). His batting average, though not the best in the league, was a fine .315, and he was the first American Leaguer in more than forty years to tally more than 400 total bases.

**TOUGH COMPETITION**

On the other hand, the voters couldn't overlook Yankee pitcher Ron Guidry. The "Ragin' Cajun" led New York to the American League pennant with 25 wins, nine shutouts, and a 1.74 earned run average, all league leaders. In 273.2 innings pitched, Guidry allowed only 187 hits, just one of them a home run, limiting opponents to a meager batting average of .193. His 25–3 record yielded a record-setting win percentage of .893.

So who was the Most Valuable Player? Voters tilted to Rice, while Guidry collected the Cy Young Award.

Competition, in baseball as in life in general, can be fierce. It's encouraging to know that God doesn't judge by the world's standards— salvation is free to all and doesn't depend on any talent or accomplishment or goodness of our own. As the apostle Paul wrote, "It is by grace you have been saved, through faith—and this not from yourselves, it is the gift of God—not by works, so that no one can boast" (Ephesians 2:8–9).

*[We] are justified freely by his grace through*
*the redemption that came by Christ Jesus.*
Romans 3:24

Professional baseball players tend to be pretty fit. But some find success in spite of their less-than-buff physiques.

*Sports Illustrated* magazine once highlighted baseball's "Well Rounded

**PHYSICAL SPECIMENS**

Players," including guys who carried approximately an eighth of a ton onto the field. The list featured Yankees superstar Babe Ruth, who in 1925 packed 256 pounds onto his 6-foot, 2-inch frame; Detroit's home run machine of the early 1990s, Cecil Fielder, 6 feet, 3 inches tall and around 260 pounds; 1990s Boston reliever Rich Garces, 6 foot even and 250 pounds; and hurler C.C. Sabathia, who weighed 260 as a Cleveland rookie in 2001 but later edged toward 300 pounds—though that's on a 6-foot, 7-inch body.

Then there was pitcher Terry Forster, once famously (and rudely) described by late-night television host David Letterman as a "fat tub of goo." Forster, officially 6 feet, 3 inches tall and 210 pounds, was fit enough to appear in 614 games over sixteen seasons with the White Sox, Pirates, Dodgers, Braves, and Angels. With Chicago in 1974, he led the American League with 24 saves and appeared in the playoffs in 1978 and '81 with Los Angeles. Not bad for a "tub of goo."

These days, much is said of the benefits of physical fitness—and even the Bible supports that idea. "Physical training is of some value," the apostle Paul wrote to Timothy (1 Timothy 4:8). But far beyond a good workout, Paul added that "godliness has value for all things, holding promise for both the present life and the life to come."

Our exercise should be both physical and spiritual. Today, do you need to get up on your feet? Or down on your knees?

*Have nothing to do with godless myths and old wives' tales; rather, train yourself to be godly.*
1 TIMOTHY 4:7

Best season ever for a pitcher? It's hard to beat the 1963 campaign of Sandy Koufax.

The Los Angeles Dodger Hall of Famer was masterful that year. At age twenty-seven, the 6-foot, 2-inch left-hander simply overwhelmed his opposition, going 25–5 for a winning percentage of .833. He started 40 games, **QUADRUPLE CROWN** completed 20, and won 11 by shutout—a southpaw record. The Brooklyn native held opposing teams to a meager .189 batting average, recording a minuscule earned run average of 1.88 and fanning 306 hitters.

Facing the mighty New York Yankees in the World Series, Koufax won the opener 5–2 with a record-setting 15 strikeouts and wrapped up an LA sweep by downing the Yanks 2–1 in Game 4. When the annual baseball awards came around, Koufax earned the first unanimous vote for the Cy Young Award and was named the National League's Most Valuable Player. And there was yet another honor, though of the mythical sort: by leading the league in wins, ERA, strikeouts, and shutouts that season, Koufax also notched baseball's "quadruple crown."

According to the apostle Paul, the Christian life is the pursuit of a crown, too: "Everyone who competes in the games goes into strict training. They do it to get a crown that will not last, but we do it to get a crown that will last forever" (1 Corinthians 9:25). What do we have to do to win? Long for Jesus' return, for one thing (2 Timothy 4:8). Persevere under trial, for another (James 1:12).

Our crowns will signify both victory and honor—and might just be a gift we'll give back to the Lord in worship.

*The twenty-four elders . . . lay their crowns before the throne and say: "You are worthy, our Lord and God, to receive glory and honor and power."*
REVELATION 4:10–11

In 1938 American League pitchers had good reason to fear Jimmie Foxx. The Boston Red Sox star finished the season with some eye-popping hitting stats—a .349 batting average, 50 home runs, and 175 runs batted in.

**PITCH AROUND HIM**

Foxx, a Hall of Famer who also played for the Cubs, Athletics, and Phillies in a twenty-year career, posted another impressive statistic in 1938. He was issued 119 walks, including a record six free passes in a June 16 game against the St. Louis Browns. Taking all of those hits and walks into account, Foxx led the league in on-base percentage that season.

Better, it seemed, to pitch around Foxx, conceding a single base than to risk the long ball. With the Boston first baseman at the plate, opposing hurlers often chose not to "play with fire."

In the book of Proverbs, Solomon used fire as a metaphor for adultery. Addressing "my son," Solomon warned against the immoral woman, the wayward wife, and the prostitute: "Can a man scoop fire into his lap without his clothes being burned? Can a man walk on hot coals without his feet being scorched? So is he who sleeps with another man's wife" (6:27–29). Better to follow the example of Joseph, who resisted the persistent advances of his master Potiphar's wife by acknowledging that sexual sin is an insult to God Himself. "And though she spoke to Joseph day after day, he refused to go to bed with her *or even be with her*" (Genesis 39:10, emphasis added).

In baseball, it's sometimes wise to pitch around a dangerous hitter. When it comes to sexual sin, avoiding that "fire" is always the best policy.

*Do not lust in your heart after her beauty*
*or let her captivate you with her eyes.*
PROVERBS 6:25

Sometimes baseball is a funny game. What else can you say when a Cleveland team, playing .500 ball in a self-described "rebuilding" season, defeats the mighty New York Yankees 22–0?

It happened in the Big Apple on August 31, 2004, as New York, entering the contest 32 games over .500, suffered its worst loss ever. The Yankees had appeared

**SKUNKED**

in five of the previous six World Series, winning three titles. They held first place in the American League East, and over the previous three years had won eight straight home games against the Tribe. But on this night, past results were no guarantee of future success.

Cleveland pitchers Jake Westbrook and Jeremy Guthrie held the Yankees scoreless on just five hits—one fewer than Cleveland shortstop Omar Vizquel had by himself, as he tied an American League record with six safeties in a nine-inning game. The Tribe notched three runs in each of the first three innings, six more in the fifth, a single tally in the sixth, and six more in the ninth to account for their historic win. In a word, the Yankees were skunked.

More than three thousand years earlier, another powerful "team" found itself in a similar predicament. Hardened Egyptian soldiers, pursuing unarmed Jewish men, women, and children, suffered a crushing defeat when God reversed His miraculous parting of the Red Sea. Jewish leader Moses commemorated the victory with a song, which went, in part, "Your right hand, LORD, was majestic in power. Your right hand, LORD, shattered the enemy" (Exodus 15:6).

God doesn't always skunk the bad guys—but He's certainly capable. That's a power that you can draw upon today.

*The Lord will rescue me from every evil attack and will bring me safely to his heavenly kingdom. To him be glory for ever and ever. Amen.*
2 TIMOTHY 4:18

In 2004 one of baseball's great streaks was broken: The Boston Red Sox snapped an eighty-six-year dry spell by winning their first World Series championship since 1918. The Chicago Cubs' record of futility, meanwhile, continued unabated.

**REBUILDING PLAN**

It's no wonder the Cubs are a sentimental favorite of so many fans. The lovable losers from Chicago's north side had last won a World Series in 1908—when Theodore Roosevelt was president. Ironically, ten years later when the Red Sox won their final championship of the twentieth century, the Cubs were their victims.

The Chicago Nationals would win pennants again in 1929, '32, '35, '38, and '45 but lose the World Series each time—to the Philadelphia Athletics, the New York Yankees, the Detroit Tigers, the Yankees, and the Tigers, respectively. After that, the Cubs sank into a prolonged slump of primarily second-division finishes, what political columnist and baseball fan George Will once called a "ninety-five-year rebuilding plan."

The Christian life, in many ways, is a long-term rebuilding plan, full of the ups and downs of a major league program. Even the great apostle Paul, converted by the direct intervention of Jesus Himself, struggled to win consistently. In Romans 7:15, he admitted, "I do not understand what I do. For what I want to do I do not do, but what I hate I do." Paul actually called himself "wretched" and cried out for a rescuer—which he found in Jesus Christ (Romans 7:25).

Like the Cubs' quest for a World Series title, our path to heavenly perfection may be long and rocky. But with Jesus in the lead, you can be sure the rebuilding plan will ultimately succeed.

*But grow in the grace and knowledge of our Lord and Savior Jesus Christ. To him be glory both now and forever!*
2 PETER 3:18

A multiple-choice test: Did San Diego's Greg Vaughn hit 20, 30, 40, or 50 home runs in 1998?

Unless you're a Padres fan, you might be surprised to learn that Vaughn slammed 50 round trippers, the most in the National League since the Reds' George Foster had 52 in 1977. But Vaughn didn't lead the league in '98—and he wasn't even close.

**UNNOTICED**

Though Vaughn's 50 homers, 119 runs batted in, and 112 runs scored helped the Friars go from worst to first in the National League West, his work was completely overshadowed by the epic home run battle between the Cardinals' Mark McGwire and the Cubs' Sammy Sosa. As they shattered Roger Maris' all-time, single season record of 61 homers, finishing with 70 and 66, respectively, Vaughn's superb season was relegated to a certain obscurity.

The San Diego left fielder's accomplishments are no less real, though, and appear in black-and-white in baseball's record books. In a similar way, our good works, though not seen or appreciated by other people, are clearly recorded and appreciated by God.

Remember Jesus' instructions in the Sermon on the Mount? When giving to the needy, "do not announce it with trumpets" (Matthew 6:2). When praying, "go into your room, close the door and pray to your Father, who is unseen" (6:6). When fasting, "put oil on your head and wash your face, so that it will not be obvious to others that you are fasting, but only to your Father" (6:17–18). Why? According to Jesus, so "your Father, who sees what is done in secret, will reward you" (6:18).

Good deeds unnoticed by others are always noticed by God. So whatever happens, do good.

*"I the LORD search the heart and examine the mind,*
*to reward each person according to their conduct,*
*according to what their deeds deserve."*
JEREMIAH 17:10

# CLAYTON KERSHAW

**Born:** March 19, 1988
**Height:** 6' 3"
**Weight:** 220 pounds
**Throws:** Left
**Bats:** Left

**Quote:** "I think it's for His glory, to make people aware that it's not something where I was lucky to throw a baseball. In Matthew, it says God gives everyone at least one talent. One guy hides his talent and gives it back, and God says, 'Cursed are you.' He doesn't want us to hide our talents; He wants us to put them in the spotlight and glorify Him. That's a pretty cool thing."

## MAJOR LEAGUE RECORD

*Drafted:* 1st round (7th overall) by Los Angeles Dodgers, 2006
*MLB debut:* May 25, 2008 (age 20), with Los Angeles Dodgers
*Stat highlights:* 21–5 record, 2.28 ERA, 248 strikeouts (2011)

In 1876, the United States' one-hundredth year, future major league pitcher Mordecai Peter Centennial Brown was born in rural Indiana.

Like many boys of that time and place, Mordecai helped on the farm—and, like an unfortunate minority, suffered a farming accident that cost him parts of two fingers. But he found he could still throw a baseball, even whip off a mean

**THREE-FINGER BROWN**

curve with his damaged right hand. In 1903 he reached the majors with the Cardinals, going 9–13 with a 2.60 earned run average.

The next season was Mordecai's first of ten with the Cubs, and the beginning of a success streak that led him to baseball's Hall of Fame. Brown won 15, 18, 26, 20, 29, 27, 25, and 21 games over the next eight seasons, racking up some league-leading figures in appearances (50 in 1909, 53 in 1911), complete games (32 in 1909, 27 in 1910), innings pitched (342.2 in 1909), and earned run average (1.04 in 1906). His years in Chicago saw the Cubs in four World Series, winning championships in 1907 and '08. Not bad for a guy they called "Three Finger" Brown.

Fingers are just one element of a pitcher's toolbox—but they were all that God needed to form the entire universe. As David wrote in the psalms, "When I consider your heavens, the work of your fingers, the moon and the stars, which you have set in place, what is mankind that you are mindful of them, human beings that you care for them?" (Psalm 8:3–4).

If God could create everything we see simply with His "fingers," how much more can He do with His whole "body"? If a problem has you stumped today, call on the finger of God for help—it's more than enough!

*Then Job replied to the LORD, "I know that you can do all things;*
*no purpose of yours can be thwarted."*
JOB 42:1–2

When it rains, an old saying goes, it pours. Just ask the Texas Rangers.

On August 22, 2007, they did something no American League team had ever done—and no major league team had done in 110 years: score 30 runs in a game.

## THE DELUGE

The Rangers, in last place in the American League West, had totaled 28 runs over their previous nine games. But against the Baltimore Orioles this night, Texas produced a deluge of 29 hits (most in the majors in fifteen years) and 30 runs (most since the Chicago Colts defeated Louisville 36–7 in 1897).

Eight Rangers drove in runs, led by the last two hitters in the lineup: Jarrod Saltalamacchia and Ramon Vazquez each had two home runs and seven RBIs. Teammates Marlon Byrd and Travis Metcalf both launched grand slams. Saltalamacchia, with four hits, increased his batting average 83 points to .262; Metcalf had been called up from the minors earlier that day. It was truly a "when it rains it pours" kind of day.

That's the way God blesses people who give. "Bring the whole tithe into the storehouse, that there may be food in my house," He said to the Old Testament Jews. "Test me in this . . . and see if I will not throw open the floodgates of heaven and pour out so much blessing that there will not be room enough to store it" (Malachi 3:10).

Though that was a challenge and promise directed to Israelites, the principle is found throughout the Bible: Give (cheerfully, as 2 Corinthians 9:7 says), and God gives back—abundantly.

> *"Give, and it will be given to you. A good measure, pressed down, shaken together and running over, will be poured into your lap. For with the measure you use, it will be measured to you."*
>
> LUKE 6:38

Poor Yogi Berra. In spite of a remarkable baseball career, he's generally remembered for his verbal bloopers.

Consider these personal statistics: Member of the Hall of Fame; catcher for fourteen pennant-winning Yankee teams; played in fifteen straight All-Star games; three-time league MVP; ranks in baseball's Top 100 in home runs (358) and RBIs (1,430); managed both New York teams to pennants—the Yankees in 1964 and the Mets in 1973.

**YOGI-SPEAK**

But Yogi's quotable gaffes are equally legendary. Here are just a few attributed to him:

- "We made too many wrong mistakes."
- "Mantle's a switch hitter because he's amphibious."
- "It gets late early out there."
- "Slump? I ain't in no slump. I just ain't hitting."

Words are powerful things. Whatever we may accomplish in life, what we say—and the way we say it—could be what defines us. Yogi Berra is remembered for his funny comments; we all know other people for their angry, untruthful, or destructive statements. Then again, we probably have fond feelings for someone whose kind, uplifting, and consoling words have helped us through hard times.

Remember this guy from Acts 4:36? "Joseph, a Levite from Cyprus, whom the apostles called Barnabas (which means 'son of encouragement')." Barnabas had developed a vocabulary of grace that showed God's love to everyone around him—and for that, he is immortalized in the pages of scripture.

Your kind words probably won't be recorded in a book of great quotations. But in the life of a needy friend, they'll qualify you as a Hall of Famer.

*Let your conversation be always full of grace, seasoned with salt,*
*so that you may know how to answer everyone.*
Colossians 4:6

Go ahead—call Rickey Henderson a thief. It's not a knock on his character but simply an acknowledgment of his prowess on the base paths.

Nobody in major league history has stolen bases like Rickey

**STEAL AWAY**

Henderson. In 1980, his second season in the majors, the Oakland speedster swiped a cool 100. His total dipped to 56 in the strike-shortened 1981 campaign, but the next year swelled to an all-time record 130, a dozen more than the previous mark set by Cardinals great Lou Brock in 1974. Baseball legend Ty Cobb, known for his aggressiveness on the base paths, had topped out at 96 steals in 1915.

The career steals trophy seems destined to sit permanently on Rickey Henderson's shelf. In 2003 Henderson's twenty-fifth major league season, the forty-four-year-old swiped three more bases to push his lifetime total to 1,406. The next man on the list, Brock, trailed by 468.

In baseball, stealing is not only acceptable, it's encouraged. That's not the case for us as Christians. God's first codified list of dos and don'ts, the Ten Commandments, included the simple rule, "You shall not steal" (Exodus 20:15). And while few of us would be tempted to rob a bank or burglarize a home, we can't forget the "smaller" temptations that might trip us up: cheating on taxes, copying movies and music, taking supplies from the office, even wasting time on the job. Though the extent may vary, stealing is stealing—and God says, "Don't."

The Christian life is not baseball . . . the steal sign is never on.

> *Anyone who has been stealing must steal no longer,*
> *but must work, doing something useful with their own hands,*
> *that they may have something to share with those in need.*
> EPHESIANS 4:28

For fifty-two years, St. Louis had two major league teams. The National League Cardinals, known early on as the Brown Stockings and Perfectos, have played uninterrupted and with considerable success since 1893.

Our focus today is on the other guys, the American League's stumbling Browns, who ultimately left town to become the Baltimore Orioles.

**ORDINARY GUYS**

The Browns got off to a good start in 1902, finishing second with a 78–58 record, five games behind the Philadelphia Athletics. But things went downhill from there. Over the next four decades, the Browns would finish as high as second only once and in third place twice. Then, in 1944, the unthinkable happened: The Browns won the American League pennant, going 89–65 to edge the Detroit Tigers by a single game.

Truth be told, World War II had given the Brownies a huge assist. With so many American League players in the armed forces, the Browns' collection of draft-deferred youngsters and old-timers rose to the occasion. Pitcher Sig Jakucki is a case in point: The man who had retired from the majors eight seasons earlier (with an 0–3 record) was seen pitching for an industrial league team and brought back to the bigs. His thirteenth victory, on the final day of the season, clinched the pennant for St. Louis.

Those wartime Browns were ordinary guys who found an opportunity to win. Sound like Jesus' disciples? One time two of them were scolded by the religious leaders of the day for preaching about Jesus, but their confident defense made a real impression: "When they saw the courage of Peter and John and realized that they were unschooled, ordinary men, they were astonished and they took note that these men had been with Jesus" (Acts 4:13).

There's nothing wrong with being an ordinary guy (or gal). The big question is, "Have you been with Jesus?"

*God chose the weak things of the world to shame the strong.*
1 CORINTHIANS 1:27

Though he once claimed, "I really didn't say everything I said," baseball's beloved master of the malaprop, Yogi Berra, does admit to uttering the phrase, "It's déjà vu all over again."

**DÉJÀ VU**

That Yogiism arose in the early 1960s, after Mickey Mantle and Roger Maris repeatedly hit back-to-back home runs for the New York Yankees. It could also apply to Major League Baseball's decision, as of the 2014 season, to implement full instant-replay review of disputed calls. (The major leagues had had limited instant-replay review—of home run calls—since 2008.)

Déjà vu is a sense of having seen something before . . . and watching just-completed plays again (and possibly over and over again) can have that effect on fans. But Yogi's "déjà vu all over again" rings true on another level, too. Sports fans may note that America's pastime is simply following the instant-replay footsteps of college football (2004), the National Basketball Association (2002), the National Hockey League (1991), and the National Football League (1986).

Instant replay is nothing new. In fact, it may be as old as Adam and Eve's disobedience to God in the Garden of Eden. Don't you think they rewound that play in their minds many times over? We know for sure that King David wrestled with instant replay; after his adultery with Bathsheba and murder of her husband, Uriah, David wrote, "I know my transgressions, and my sin is always before me" (Psalm 51:3).

That kind of instant replay is called "conscience." But once we admit our sin to God—"Against you, you only have I sinned and done what is evil in your sight" (Psalm 51:4)—He forgives our sin and allows us to move on. We don't ever need to replay or review it again!

> *"I, even I, am he who blots out your transgressions,*
> *for my own sake, and remembers your sins no more."*
> ISAIAH 43:25

Simply reading the box score, one would never imagine the drama of a game played on August 16, 1920, between New York and Cleveland.

All of the typical statistical shorthand—AB, H, R, DP, LOB—appears as it has in literally tens of thousands of box scores over the long history of Major League Baseball. There's also the brief notation, "HBP: Chapman (by Mays)," indicating that Indians batter Ray Chapman was hit by a pitch thrown by Yankees starter Carl Mays.

**HIT BY PITCH**

Though the notation is dispassionate, the event was horrifying. Mays' submarine-style pitch sailed up and in on the popular Cleveland shortstop, hitting him in the left temple. In those days before batting helmets, Chapman's skull was fractured. He crumpled to the ground and would die early the next morning. Chapman became the only major leaguer to be killed playing the game.

At age twenty-nine, Ray Chapman was just doing his job when disaster struck. Jesus once told a parable of another man conducting his business, unaware that "this very night your life will be demanded from you" (Luke 12:20). In sharing the story of a rich man whose abundant crops prompted him to think, "Take life easy; eat, drink and be merry" (Luke 12:19), Jesus was warning against greed. But the parable also dramatically points out the uncertainty of life. Who among us knows when a car crash, a heart attack, or even a pitched baseball might send us into eternity?

The only true preparation for death is accepting Jesus Christ as Savior. If this were your day, would you be ready?

*What is your life? You are a mist that appears*
*for a little while and then vanishes.*
JAMES 4:14

Pitchers strive for "location," placing a baseball where opposing batters are least likely to hit it. But good location had another meaning for San Francisco hurler Billy Pierce. In 1962 it was all about the ballpark he played in.

**NO PLACE LIKE HOME**

The Detroit-born southpaw began his career with the hometown Tigers in 1945. After a couple years out of the majors, Pierce returned to the Tigers in 1948 then moved on to Chicago, where he was a six-time All-Star in twelve seasons with the White Sox.

In 1962 Pierce headed west to San Francisco, going 16–6 for the Giants. His solid performance helped the Bay Area Nationals win the pennant but was also memorable for the perfect 12–0 record he enjoyed at Candlestick Park. That was a single-season record for most home wins without a loss.

For Billy Pierce in '62, there was truly no place like home. How much truer that will be for Christians in eternity.

"My Father's house has many rooms," Jesus once told His disciples; "if that were no so, would I have told you that I am going there to prepare a place for you? And if I go and prepare a place for you, I will come back and take you to be with me that you also may be where I am" (John 14:2–3).

A perfect place forever, filled with the love and wonders of God, without any of the problems of sin—it just doesn't get any better than that.

Are you headed toward home?

*Thomas said to him, "Lord, we don't know where you are going, so how can we know the way?" Jesus answered, "I am the way and the truth and the life. No one comes to the Father except through me."*
JOHN 14:5–6

It was the kind of season that inspires movies: the bumbling losers get their act together and win it all. For the New York Mets, the year was 1969.

As a replacement for New York's recently departed Dodgers and Giants, the Mets got off to a typical expansion-team start in 1962. Finishing 40–120, a whopping 60½ games behind first-place San Francisco, they were dubbed

**MIRACLE METS**

"My Amazin's" by manager Casey Stengel. Through 1968, the Mets never finished higher than ninth in the ten-team National League.

In the first year of divisional play, though, manager Gil Hodges led the Mets to a 27-game turnaround from the previous year, as they won the National League East with a 100–62 record. Breezing through the postseason, New York dispatched Atlanta in three games then shocked the powerful Baltimore Orioles in the World Series four games to one. Some called the Mets' play miraculous.

By definition, miracles are rare. It's not often that a team accomplishes what the 1969 Mets did—nor is it every day that a serious health problem is cured, unexpected money fixes a financial squeeze, or a broken relationship is restored. But even if rare, miracles do happen. Remember Sarah having baby Isaac at age ninety? Or the sun standing still to help Joshua's army defeat its enemies? Or Jesus rising from the dead?

As Christians, we should expect to see some miracles in our daily lives. Large or small, those unexpected blessings remind us of God's power to turn a bad season good.

*"Is anything too hard for the LORD?"*
GENESIS 18:14

Rogers Hornsby loved to play baseball—and it showed.

The Hall of Famer started a twenty-three-year big league career in St. Louis in 1915, playing a dozen seasons for the Cardinals. Over the next

**AWAITING THE RETURN** eleven years, he would appear in the uniforms of the New York Giants, Boston Braves, Chicago Cubs, St. Louis Browns, and briefly, the Cardinals once again.

"Rajah," as he was known, was primarily a middle infielder, best known for playing second base.

Hornsby is in or near the Top 100 players of all time in games played (2,259), at bats (8,173), and home runs (301); and in or near the Top 30 in hits (2,930), doubles (541), triples (169), and total bases (4,712). And he was efficient with all of those hits: Rajah's career batting average of .358 is second only to Ty Cobb's .366.

Baseball provided meaning for Rogers Hornsby's life. "People ask me what I do in winter when there's no baseball," he was once quoted as saying. "I'll tell you what I do. I stare out the window and wait for spring."

Christians should have a similar anticipation—but with Jesus as the object. The apostle Paul, offering pastoral advice to his protégé Titus, encouraged self-control "while we wait for the blessed hope—the appearing of the glory of our great God and Savior, Jesus Christ, who gave himself for us to redeem us from all wickedness and to purify for himself a people that are his very own, eager to do what is good" (Titus 2:13–14).

The annual return of baseball is fun. The coming return of Christ should change our lives.

*And now, dear children, continue in him, so that when he appears we may be confident and unashamed before him at his coming.*
1 JOHN 2:28

# ALBERT PUJOLS

**Born:** January 16, 1980
**Height:** 6' 3"
**Weight:** 230 pounds
**Throws:** Right
**Bats:** Right

**Quote:** "You think I'm going to ruin my relationship with God just because I want to get better in this game? You think I'm going to ruin everything because of steroids? I want to be the person who represents God, represents my family, and represents [my team] the right way."

## MAJOR LEAGUE RECORD

*Drafted:* 13th round by St. Louis Cardinals, 1999

*MLB debut:* April 2, 2001 (age 21) with St. Louis Cardinals

*Stat highlights:* .359 batting average (2003), 51 doubles (2003, 2004), 49 home runs, 137 RBIs (2006)

Harmon Killebrew swung a big stick—all the way to Cooperstown.

A burly slugger who carried more than 210 pounds on his 5-foot, 11-inch frame, Killebrew broke into the majors in 1954 with the Washington Senators. But the "monumental home run and RBI success" memorialized on Killebrew's Hall of Fame plaque wasn't immediately apparent. The man from Payette, Idaho, played sparingly his first five seasons, recording only 11 home runs and 30 runs batted in.

**BIG JOBS, LITTLE JOBS**

Killebrew's breakout season was 1959, when he played in 153 games, swatted a league-leading 42 home runs, and notched 105 RBIs. In twelve of the next thirteen seasons, he would hit at least 25 home runs, registering more than 40 in seven of those years. His 1962–64 totals of 48, 45, and 49, respectively, were all league highs, as were his 44 in 1967 and 49 in 1969, when he was named American League MVP. Overall, Killebrew slammed 573 home runs, within the Top 10 of all time.

The long ball was clearly Harmon Killebrew's thing—in 8,147 career at bats, the man nicknamed "Killer" recorded not a single bunt hit or sacrifice bunt. Perhaps the bunt seemed like lowly work to a man accustomed to clearing the fences.

In the Christian realm, there's no such thing as "lowly work." Jesus showed that by washing His disciples' feet, a job typically handled by servants. "Now that I, your Lord and Teacher, have washed your feet, you also should wash one another's feet," Jesus said. "I have set you an example that you should do as I have done for you" (John 13:14–15).

Willingness to perform the "small jobs" indicates a heart ready for greater service. Are you willing today?

> *"If anyone gives even a cup of cold water to one of these little ones who is my disciple, truly I tell you, that person will certainly not lose their reward."*
> MATTHEW 10:42

Baseball is a game of perfect proportions. But it wasn't always that way.

In the major leagues' early days, rule makers often changed the figures modern fans take for granted. In 1887, for example, batters were given *four* strikes and needed *five* balls to take a walk. Also that year, pitchers were required to keep one foot on the back of the "pitcher's box," eliminating the hops, skips, and running starts with which some hurlers enhanced their deliveries. The one-step rule established a more consistent pitching distance of 55 feet, 6 inches.

**CHANGES**

In 1888 the three-strikes-and-you're-out rule was restored, to the notable benefit of pitchers. The National League's seasonal earned run average fell from 4.05 to 2.83, while the batting average dipped 27 points. Shortstop Monte Ward, of the champion New York Giants, saw his batting average plummet to .251, from .338 the year before.

With the 1889 season, walks were again awarded after four balls, and in 1893, the pitching distance was lengthened to its current 60 feet, 6 inches. That last change, plus the introduction of the pitcher's rubber, meant grief for many hurlers and caused offensive production to rise—by almost one and a half runs per game in the League Association.

Change can be tough whether you're a major league player or the average fan. A downsizing, a relocation, a family addition, or the loss of a loved one can cause stress and confusion. But it's good to know that one thing—or, more accurately, one Person—never changes: "In the beginning you laid the foundations of the earth, and the heavens are the work of your hands. They will perish, but you remain. . . . Like clothing you will change them and they will be discarded. But you remain the same" (Psalm 102:25–27).

In a world of change, you have a God who doesn't. When life gets crazy, hold on to Him!

*Jesus Christ is the same yesterday and today and forever.*
Hebrews 13:8

In early 2004, many baseball fans scratched their heads when catcher Ivan Rodriguez signed with the Detroit Tigers.

Both an All-Star and a Gold Glove winner ten times over, Rodriguez had months earlier led the Florida Marlins to a World Series championship, earning the postseason MVP award along the way. Now he was joining a team with a ten-year streak of losing records—including the American League's all-time worst 119 defeats in 2003.

**FIRST TO WORST**

Rodriguez told reporters he didn't think of Detroit as a "losing team." Rather, they were a team that "just had a bad season." It was a positive perspective, one perhaps colored by the $40 million contract he received from the Tigers. But to many fans, Rodriguez's jump from first to worst just didn't make sense.

In the same way, to many Christians, God's decisions often confuse and perplex. Why does He allow evil in the world? Why do faithful Christians face trials and persecution? Why didn't God answer that really important prayer you prayed over and over again?

We may never get completely satisfying answers to those questions. But when we take on faith that "God is love" (1 John 4:8) and that "in all things God works for the good of those who love him, who have been called according to his purpose" (Romans 8:28), we have to believe that He has a good purpose in the seemingly unexplainable.

Ivan Rodriguez had his reasons in signing with Detroit. Trust that God has much bigger reasons for everything else.

*"As the heavens are higher than the earth, so are my ways higher than your ways and my thoughts than your thoughts."*

ISAIAH 55:9

Pure baseball ability isn't the only thing that endears Roberto Clemente to fans of the game.

Of course, he had plenty of talent. The native Puerto Rican played eighteen years in the majors, entirely with the Pittsburgh Pirates, compiling exactly 3,000 career hits. He led the National League in batting average in 1961 (.351),

**ABOVE AND BEYOND**

1964 (.339), 1965 (.329), and 1967 (.357), finishing with a lifetime figure of .317. Primarily a right fielder, Clemente was known for a strong throwing arm and won twelve straight Gold Glove awards from 1961 to 1972. He helped the Bucs to four postseason appearances and two World Series titles—exciting 4–3 decisions over the Yankees in 1960 and the Orioles in 1971.

But Roberto Clemente went above and beyond the game of baseball. Responding to an earthquake in Nicaragua, the Pirate outfielder personally joined a relief effort—and died, December 31, 1972, in the crash of a supply plane. He was elected to the Hall of Fame the very next year on a special ballot.

Going "above and beyond" for others is the theme of one of Jesus' most famous parables. In that story, a Jewish man attacked by robbers and left for dead is ignored by two religious leaders but pitied by a man of Samaria—an ethnic group the Jews shunned. This "good Samaritan" cleaned and bandaged the victim's wounds, helped him onto a donkey, and took him to an inn. Then the Samaritan paid the innkeeper to continue the man's care and promised to reimburse any extra expenses incurred. Jesus concluded his talk with a command: "Go and do likewise" (Luke 10:37).

Needy people are all around us. Will you go above and beyond to serve them?

*You, my brothers and sisters, were called to be free. But do not use your freedom to indulge the flesh; rather, serve one another humbly in love.*
GALATIANS 5:13

Baseball playing brothers occasionally meet on the field. But the Underwood boys took the idea of "sibling rivalry" a step further in 1979.

The sons of former minor league pitcher John Underwood, Tom and Pat played for Toronto and

## BROTHER VERSUS BROTHER

Detroit, respectively. The elder Tom had just passed the midpoint of an eleven-year major league career; kid brother Pat was a newly minted rookie. By nature or nurture, both boys had followed in Dad's footsteps—right up to the pitching mound.

On the last day of May, Pat got his first starting assignment—against his own big brother. Tom, coming off a 6–14 season with the second-year Blue Jays, pitched a beauty. His complete game was marred only by the eighth inning home run of the Tigers' Jerry Morales.

Unfortunately for Tom, little sib Pat went 8⅓ scoreless innings and earned the victory. We can hope their family rivalry was good natured, both on the field and afterward—when young bucks are apt to remind an older brother of such a result over and over again.

Jesus once warned about real family tension, the kind He Himself might create: "Do you think I came to bring peace on earth? No, I tell you, but division. From now on there will be five in one family divided against each other, three against two and two against three. They will be divided, father against son and son against father" (Luke 12:51–53). Why? Because not everyone accepts Jesus' message of faith and repentance.

If your Christianity has caused tension in a relationship, don't take it personally. Keep showing love and kindness as best you can, and pray that God will change the other person's heart.

*Some of the Pharisees said, "This man is not from God,*
*for he does not keep the Sabbath." But others asked,*
*"How can a sinner perform such signs?" So they were divided.*
JOHN 9:16

When is a home run not a home run? When baseball's official rules say so.

In the early twentieth century—before Babe Ruth wore Yankee pinstripes—players could not hit game-winning home runs if there were runners on base. Even if a batter slammed a ball over the fence, he would be credited with just enough hit to push the winning run across the plate.

**THE RULES**

That rule quirk snatched a homer from the Bambino, then with the Red Sox, in 1918. Batting in the bottom of the tenth, in a scoreless tie against Cleveland, Ruth crushed a Stan Coveleskie pitch into Fenway's bleachers. But the shot was ruled a triple, since that was all Ruth needed to drive home Amos Strunk from first.

To some, the rule seemed unfair. One Boston sportswriter argued, "The longest and most beautifully executed skyscraper [Ruth] has ever delivered in the home town of his team should be scored for what it really was," railing against "the black-hearted injustice in the scoring rules as they stand."

We all face unfair and irritating rules—many of them demands of our government. But God's Word is clear: We're to obey whether we like them or not. Remember Jesus' words to the Pharisees, trying to trap Him with a question about paying taxes? "So give back to Caesar what is Caesar's, and to God what is God's" (Matthew 22:21).

In a free society, we can work to change the rules—that homer/no homer provision was modified in 1920. But the rules as they stand should be obeyed.

*Let everyone be subject to the governing authorities, for there is no authority except that which God has established. . . . Whoever rebels against the authority is rebelling against what God has instituted, and those who do so will bring judgment on themselves.*
Romans 13:1–2

Baseball is a young man's game? The 1983 Phillies turned that idea on its head.

Philadelphia won the National League East pennant with a veteran

**WHEEZE KIDS**

lineup featuring several players in their late thirties and early forties. Starting pitcher Steve Carlton, in his nineteenth major league season, won 15 games and led the league in innings pitched (283.2) at age thirty-eight. Reliever Tug McGraw, star of the 1980 World Series, contributed 55.2 innings as a thirty-nine-year-old.

Then there were three members of Cincinnati's old Big Red Machine, winding down their careers in the City of Brotherly Love. Second baseman Joe Morgan, who turned forty in September, appeared in 123 games and hit 16 home runs; first baseman Tony Perez, celebrating birthday forty-one in May, played 91 games and notched 43 RBIs; and "Charlie Hustle," Pete Rose, having celebrated his forty-second birthday in April, batted .245 in 151 games.

Nicknamed the "Wheeze Kids," the elder corps helped the Phils to their second World Series appearance in four seasons. All in all, the old guys turned in a very respectable performance.

Age and respect should go together, though that doesn't happen automatically—it takes a conscious effort on our part. As the apostle Paul told Titus, respectability is actually something to be taught: "Teach the older men to be temperate, worthy of respect, self-controlled, and sound in faith, in love and in endurance" (Titus 2:2).

Whether we consider ourselves "older men," the fact is that we're each getting older every day. The more important issue is this: Are you learning to be better?

> . . . until we all reach unity in the faith and in the
> knowledge of the Son of God and become mature,
> attaining to the whole measure of the fullness of Christ.
> EPHESIANS 4:13

How times have changed.

In an era of multimillion-dollar sports contracts, it's hard to imagine baseball players earning far less breathtaking amounts of money. But there was a time when Honus Wagner, the Hall of Fame shortstop who starred from 1897 to 1917, reportedly said he would not play a season for "a penny less than $1,500."

**WAGE SCALE**

Shortly after World War II, baseball's first six-figure player appeared. Hank Greenberg, Detroit's star home run hitter, had served in the military for four full years, returning to the game halfway through the 1945 season. In 1947, Greenberg's final baseball campaign, he set a milestone by earning over $100,000 with the Pittsburgh Pirates.

More than thirty years would pass before a major leaguer broke the million-dollar mark for a season. The lucky (and talented) free agent pitcher Nolan Ryan, lured from the California Angels by the Houston Astros, inked the first seven-figure contract.

And then there's Alex Rodriguez, who signed a ten-year deal worth more than a quarter billion (yes, *billion* with a *b*) dollars in 2000. The Texas Rangers made that offer, though three years later they sent A-Rod to New York where the Yankees could pay his $25–27 million annual salaries.

While baseball's wage scale has increased dramatically over the years, the "wages of sin," to use a biblical phrase, remain the same: death (see Romans 6:23). Since "all have sinned" (Romans 3:23), everyone can expect a depressing payday. Don't overlook the second half of Romans 6:23, though: "but the gift of God is eternal life in Christ Jesus our Lord."

That's not a wage to be earned but a gift to be accepted. Have you taken yours?

*He . . . asked, "Sirs, what must I do to be saved?" They replied,*
*"Believe in the Lord Jesus, and you will be saved."*
Acts 16:30–31

You could never accuse Wilbur Wood of laziness.

As a pitcher for the Chicago White Sox, the 6-foot lefty racked up some astonishing endurance marks. For three straight seasons, from 1968

**TIRELESS**

through 1970, Wood led the American League in mound appearances, including a major league record 88 to start the string. Those appearances were almost entirely in relief, but Wood was soon moved to the starting rotation, where he continued his tireless throwing.

From 1972 through 1975, the Cambridge, Massachusetts, native led the league in games started, with 49 (most in the majors in 64 years), 48, 42, and 43, respectively. In 1972 and '73, he had the most innings pitched of any American League hurler (376.2 and 359.1), and in the latter season became the first major league pitcher in more than half a century to both win and lose at least 20 games. Wood went 24–20 for a White Sox team that finished 77–85, in fifth place in the American League West.

Hard work was Wilbur Wood's trademark—as it should be for Christians, too. God put the very first man in the Garden of Eden "to work it and take care of it" (Genesis 2:15). In eternity, around Jesus' throne, "his servants will serve him" (Revelation 22:3). In between, the Bible often speaks of the virtues—and the rewards—of good, hard, honest work.

Though overwork can bring its own problems, laziness is clearly a no-no for Christians. Is there some job you should be attending to today?

*All hard work brings a profit,*
*but mere talk leads only to poverty.*
PROVERBS 14:23

Prospects were bright for the Detroit Tigers and their new president, Frank Navin.

With a young Ty Cobb leading the way, the Motor City boys won their first-ever pennant in 1907 then duplicated that feat in each of the next two years. Detroit slipped to third in 1910, but when Navin arrived the next season, he expected plenty of championships to come. He was to be disappointed.

**THE ULTIMATE**

The Tigers plummeted to sixth place in 1912 and stayed there the following season. Their fortunes turned upward in 1915 when they won 100 games—but the Red Sox won 101, and Detroit wound up second. Another runner-up finish in 1923 was the best the Tigers could do till they finally won their next pennant in 1934, more than two decades after Navin's arrival.

Unfortunately for Detroit, the Tigers lost the 1934 World Series in seven games to St. Louis. Everything did come together in 1935, though: the Bengals edged the New York Yankees for the American League pennant then downed the Chicago Cubs in six games for their first World Series title. Navin, having finally seen the ultimate, died later that year.

Frank Navin's story is reminiscent of a biblical character who had truly seen "the ultimate"—Jesus. A devout man named Simeon had been told by the Holy Spirit "that he would not die before he had seen the Lord's Messiah" (Luke 2:26). When the elderly saint held the baby Jesus at the temple, he praised God, saying, "Sovereign Lord, as you have promised, you may now dismiss your servant in peace" (Luke 2:29). After seeing Jesus, there was nothing more Simeon could want.

Shouldn't the same be true for you?

*"My eyes have seen your salvation, which you have prepared in the sight of all nations."*
LUKE 2:30–31

# CARLOS BELTRAN

**Born:** April 24, 1977
**Height:** 6' 1"
**Weight:** 215 pounds
**Throws:** Right
**Bats:** Both

**Quote:** "It's good to have a big house and a nice car, but it's better when you have Jesus in your heart. He's more important than anything. I pray every day when I wake up and while I'm driving to the ballpark. I try to read the Bible and memorize it and think about it the whole game."

## MAJOR LEAGUE RECORD

*Drafted:* 2nd round by Kansas City Royals, 1995

*MLB debut:* September 14, 1998 (age 21), with Kansas City Royals

*Stat highlights:* 41 home runs, 38 doubles, 116 RBIs, .275 batting average, 2006 with New York Mets

In a long and productive major league career, Norm Cash accomplished much—377 career home runs, four All-Star selections, three postseason appearances. But he's in the record books for a big slump.

The seventeen-year veteran broke into the big leagues in 1958, appearing in 13 games with the Chicago White Sox. He found his true home with the Tigers

## THE BIG SLUMP

in 1960, playing the rest of his career—through 1974—in the Motor City. Primarily a first baseman, Cash appeared in more than 2,000 big league games, recording more than 6,700 at bats, more than 1,800 hits, and a career batting average of .271.

Offensively, Cash put everything together his second year in Detroit. Playing in the first 162-game season of the expansion era, the Texas native appeared in 159 games, smashing a league-leading 193 hits for a first-place batting average of .361—37 points higher than the runner-up, Tiger teammate Al Kaline.

The next season was a different story, though—Cash played 11 fewer games and had 28 fewer at bats, but 70 fewer hits—and his batting average plummeted to .243. The 118-point drop was the largest ever for a batting title winner from one year to the next.

We as Christians need to guard against similar slumps—in our commitment to God and His Word, in our private behavior, and in our example to a watching world. In the words of the apostle Paul, "I urge you to live a life worthy of the calling you have received" (Ephesians 4:1).

A spiritual slump—of any size—is a big problem.

*Join with me in suffering for the gospel, by the power of God. He has saved us and called us to a holy life.*
2 TIMOTHY 1:8–9

Fans did a lot of wincing when Pete Reiser played the game.

The reaction had nothing to do with the Brooklyn outfielder's skills—in 1941, his first full season, the twenty-two-year-old Reiser led the National

## SACRIFICING HIS BODY

League in batting average (.343), slugging average (.558), runs (117), doubles (39), and triples (17). What made the spectators flinch was Reiser's propensity for injury.

Consider these major mishaps: Reiser is carried away on a stretcher after a 1941 beaning that prompts the Dodgers to begin wearing plastic batting helmets. Reiser suffers a skull fracture when he runs into an outfield wall in 1942. Reiser breaks an ankle with two weeks to go in the 1946 campaign. Injuries were a way of life for Pete Reiser, who averaged only 86 games a season over his ten years in the big leagues.

For the game of baseball, Pete Reiser was willing to sacrifice his body. That's exactly the picture the apostle Paul once drew for Christians living in Rome.

In the first eleven chapters of the book of Romans, Paul goes into great detail explaining salvation as a gift from God—completely undeserved by those who receive it. Then in chapter 12, he says, "Therefore"—because of everything he's just said—"I urge you, brothers and sisters, in view of God's mercy, to offer your bodies as a living sacrifice, holy and pleasing to God—this is your true and proper worship" (Romans 12:1).

As Christians, ease and comfort aren't our goals. Take Pete Reiser's lead and give yourself up for the cause.

> *You also, like living stones, are being built into a spiritual house to be a holy priesthood, offering spiritual sacrifices acceptable to God through Jesus Christ.*
>
> 1 PETER 2:5

Today's baseball quiz: Who was Enzo Hernandez?

If you followed baseball closely in the 1970s, you might possibly recall him. If the San Diego Padres are your team, you may have some recollection of the Venezuelan shortstop. But casual fans probably have little memory of the man.

**POWER SHORTAGE**

On a string of second-division Padres teams—including three that lost 100 or more games—Hernandez prowled the territory between second and third base. He appeared in 143 games in 1971, his rookie year, and played in as many as 147 games for San Diego three seasons later.

He was never an offensive threat, posting a lifetime batting average of .224 and exactly *two* home runs in 2,327 career at bats. For players with more than 500 at bats in a season, his 1971 campaign went down as one of the worst ever in terms of run production. In his 549 opportunities, the Padres' shortstop recorded only 12 RBIs.

Compared to the heavy hitters of his time—the Reggie Jacksons, the Willie Stargells, and the Hank Aarons—Enzo Hernandez was weak. Take that image several steps further, to *powerless*, and you have the apostle Paul's description of all people apart from Jesus.

"At just the right time, when we were still powerless, Christ died for the ungodly," Paul wrote in Romans 5:6. But Jesus' sacrifice demonstrated God's love for humanity (see Romans 5:8) and gives you a chance to tap into the greatest power source ever—God Himself.

*I am not ashamed of the gospel, because it is the power*
*of God that brings salvation to everyone who believes:*
*first to the Jew, then to the Gentile.*
ROMANS 1:16

Imagine yourself a manager, filling out this lineup card: Ty Cobb in center field, Babe Ruth in right, Honus Wagner at short, Cy Young on the mound. . . .

**THE INDUCTION**

It never happened on the field, but in 1939, those superstars—along with pitchers Walter Johnson and Grover Cleveland Alexander, outfielder Tris Speaker, and second baseman Eddie Collins—came together as members of the very first class of the Hall of Fame.

Consider these statistics: The three pitchers mentioned had a combined 1,301 victories and 8,510 strikeouts. Cobb and Speaker, center fielding rivals in the early twentieth century, combined for 7,703 hits, with lifetime batting averages of .366 and .345, respectively. Middle infielders Wagner and Collins were known for their slick defense and their hitting prowess— they had 6,735 hits between them, finishing with career averages of .328 and .333, respectively. Ruth, of course, was in a class by himself with 714 home runs, and a career slugging percentage of .690.

Fans who had cheered the stars' on-field exploits got another chance to applaud when each was inducted into the new baseball shrine in Cooperstown, New York. It was, it seemed, a bit of baseball heaven.

In the real heaven, where God Himself lives, there's cheering on a much grander scale—but not for a select few baseball heroes. "There is rejoicing in the presence of the angels of God," Jesus said, "over one sinner who repents" (Luke 15:10). That's an induction ceremony with eternal ramifications.

Are you in the lineup?

> *You make known to me the path of life; you will fill me with joy in your presence, with eternal pleasures at your right hand.*
> PSALM 16:11

For every All-Star, there are dozens of nonstars.

No disrespect is intended, of course. But the reality is that a handful of ballplayers rise above their peers, gaining the lion's share of praise—and the monster contracts. Many more players toil in relative obscurity.

**NON-STARS**

For every pitcher like Tom Seaver (twenty seasons, 311 wins, elected to the Hall of Fame in his first year of eligibility), there are many more like Scipio Spinks (seven career victories with the Astros and Cardinals, 1969–73). For every infielder like Mike Schmidt (eighteen seasons, 548 home runs, Hall of Famer on his first ballot), there are scores of players like shortstop Buddy Biancalana (six home runs, .205 batting average for the Royals and Astros, 1982–87).

Human nature aspires to stardom. But stars are, by definition, unusual—so most people won't be. Is that a problem? Not at all. Because they're so few in number, stars need the nonstars to achieve their team goals. Everyone counts.

It's no different in the Christian world. Consider the church's beginning in the book of Acts: "Peter stood up with the Eleven, raised his voice and addressed the crowd. . . . Those who accepted his message were baptized, and about three thousand were added to their number that day" (Acts 2:14, 41). We know very little of those three thousand people—but those "nonstars" comprise the foundation of the church we enjoy today.

If you're one of the world's stars, great. If not, don't worry. You're in good company.

*Brothers and sisters, think of what you were when you were called. Not many of you were wise by human standards; not many were influential; not many were of noble birth. . . . Therefore, as it is written: "Let the one who boasts boast in the Lord."*

1 CORINTHIANS 1:26, 31

They labor in relative obscurity, taking heat from both players and fans. But what would baseball be without umpires?

Even the game's official rule book has admitted that the umpire's job

**PASSING JUDGMENT**

"is often a trying position." They are given responsibility for the conduct of the game and for maintaining "discipline and order on the playing field"—not always an easy task when faced with a crowd of young, aggressive, highly paid, and very competitive ballplayers.

The umpire's job is to enforce the written rules of the game, which often come down to an "either/or" determination. Was a pitched ball a strike or not? Was a runner safe or out? Did a batted ball land fair or foul? Is a player's uniform complete or incomplete? Keeping a game equitable for both teams comes down to good judgment.

The area of judgment can be a tricky one for us as believers. Most everyone, Christian or not, is familiar with Jesus' words in the Sermon on the Mount: "Do not judge, or you too will be judged" (Matthew 7:1). But the apostle Paul, writing about an immoral member of the church in Corinth, said, "I have already passed judgment in the name of our Lord Jesus on the one who has been doing this" (1 Corinthians 5:3).

Is that a contradiction? No—if you look at Paul as a baseball umpire, holding up the questionable actions of a professing Christian against the rule book of the Bible: Did that man's life conform to scripture or not? Jesus' words, on the other hand, seem to deal with judging others' motives—or criticizing others for sins that we ourselves might be committing.

Is this a day for judging your own judgments?

*Judge nothing before the appointed time; wait until the Lord comes. He will bring to light what is hidden in darkness and will expose the motives of the heart.*
1 CORINTHIANS 4:5

Kevin Kouzmanoff experienced the dream. Casey Blake provided the reality.

On September 2, 2006, the two men became Cleveland teammates when Kouzmanoff was called up to the bigs from Triple A Buffalo. Only hours after reporting, Kouzmanoff, with his new Indian comrades, was playing in Texas.

**NOT THAT EASY**

Batting seventh, in place of injured designated hitter Travis Hafner, Kouzmanoff stepped into a first-inning, bases-loaded situation. Tribe players urged a Hafner-like result for the rookie—the regular designated hitter had already tied a major league record with six grand slams in '06—and the young Kouzmanoff electrified the Cleveland bench by smashing Edinson Volquez's first offering over the center field fence. Kouzmanoff was the third player in major league history to hit a grand slam in his initial at bat, the only one to accomplish the feat on the first pitch he saw.

Blake, the Indians' right fielder, caught Kouzmanoff in the dugout afterward. Speaking from eight years' major league experience, Blake reminded the rookie, "Hey, Kouz, it's not that easy up here all the time."

Isn't that true of life? For every high, it seems, there's at least one low—a broken relationship, a health scare, persecution, you name it. Sometimes the lows come in bunches, and often they're worst when we're trying our best. "We must go through many hardships to enter the kingdom of God," Paul and Barnabas told Christians in Asia Minor (Acts 14:22b). But quitting is no option: The two missionaries spent time "strengthening the disciples and encouraging them to remain true to the faith" (Acts 14:22a).

When life gets hard, think of the benefits of heaven. Stay true to your faith!

*"Do not be afraid of what you are about to suffer.... Be faithful,*
*even to the point of death, and I will give you life as your victor's crown."*
REVELATION 2:10

Look carefully at Minnie Minoso's career statistics, and you'll find something amazing: the Havana native played major league ball in *five* different decades.

**NEVER TOO OLD**

After three seasons with the Negro League's New York Cubans, Minoso joined the Cleveland Indians in 1949. From 1951 to 1964, he played in Cleveland, Chicago, St. Louis, and Washington. After the 1964 season, he "retired"—for twelve years.

In 1976, at age fifty-three, Minoso was back in a White Sox uniform, slapping a single in eight at bats to become the second-oldest major leaguer ever to get a hit. Four years later, he played in two more games for the White Sox, becoming, at age fifty-seven, the oldest player ever to attempt an at bat.

"You're never too old" seemed to be Minoso's philosophy. He would have found a kindred spirit in the Bible's Caleb, one of only two Israelites to survive forty years in the wilderness and enter the Promised Land.

"Here I am today, eighty-five years old!" Caleb said on the border of Canaan. "I am still as strong today as the day Moses sent me out; I'm just as vigorous to go out to battle now as I was then. Now give me this hill country that the LORD promised me that day" (Joshua 14:10–12).

Who's to say what "too old" is? Whether you're twenty, forty, or eighty-five, is there a new challenge you should tackle? Maybe it's teaching a Sunday school class or joining a short-term missions team. Maybe it's restoring a broken relationship or improving your marriage. Maybe it's [your challenge here].

Find your own hill country to conquer. You're never too old.

> *"Even to your old age and gray hairs I am he, I am he who will sustain you. I have made you and I will carry you; I will sustain you and I will rescue you."*
> ISAIAH 46:4

Though it never rose to the Hall of Fame level, Al Downing's major league career boasted certain successes.

Over seventeen years, Downing pitched for four teams: the Yankees, A's, Brewers, and Dodgers. Along the way, he recorded a 20-win season and led the National League with five shutouts (with Los Angeles in 1971), led the American

**LEGACIES, PART 1**

League in strikeouts (217 for New York in '64), and pitched in three World Series (1963 and '64 with the Yankees, 1974 with the Dodgers).

But Al Downing is probably best remembered as the answer to a baseball trivia question: What pitcher served up Hank Aaron's 715th round tripper, allowing the Braves' slugger to surpass Babe Ruth as baseball's all-time home run king? That happened on April 8, 1974, creating an enduring legacy for the man from Trenton, New Jersey.

For Al Downing, a solid baseball career was overshadowed by a single pitch—just as the otherwise positive lives of two Bible characters were colored by certain negative events. Who can forget King David's sin with Bathsheba (2 Samuel 11) or Noah's embarrassing episode with drunkenness (Genesis 9)?

The shield against that kind of failure is wisdom. "Do not forsake wisdom, and she will protect you," Solomon wrote in the Proverbs; "love her, and she will watch over you" (Proverbs 4:6). The psalm writer described just where that valuable commodity can be found: "The fear of the LORD is the beginning of wisdom" (Psalm 111:10).

How would you like to be remembered? Be sure to build your legacy on the solid foundation of God's Word.

*Your statutes are my heritage forever;*
*they are the joy of my heart.*
PSALM 119:111

Sometimes individual achievements outshine a player's career as a whole. Consider, for example, the story of Kurt Bevacqua.

By most any measurement, the Miami Beach native was a mediocre

hitter. Over a fifteen-year major league career, he batted .236 in limited playing time with the Indians, Royals, Pirates, Brewers, Rangers, and Padres. Bevacqua, who appeared at every position but pitcher, catcher, and center field, averaged only 65 games a season, playing a career-high 114 with San Diego in 1979.

In 1984, his next-to-last major league campaign, Bevacqua was part of his only pennant-winning team. He played in 59 games for the Padres, batted .200, and hit one of his 27 career home runs before San Diego manager Dick Williams made Bevacqua a surprise choice as World Series designated hitter. Though Detroit would win the Fall Classic four games to one, Bevacqua would turn in a memorable performance, batting .412, recording four RBIs, and smacking two home runs—including the game winner in San Diego's sole victory.

It was a late breakthrough, not unlike that of a biblical character who found salvation at the eleventh hour. Recall the criminal beside Jesus, who went from mocking the Lord to begging, "Remember me when you come into your kingdom"? Jesus, of course, honored the man's request, telling him, "Today you will be with me in paradise" (Luke 23:42–43).

It's never too late to do something good, whether that's accepting Christ, restoring a relationship, finding a place of service—you name it. What legacy should you be building today?

*I have chosen the way of faithfulness;*
*I have set my heart on your laws.*
PSALM 119:30

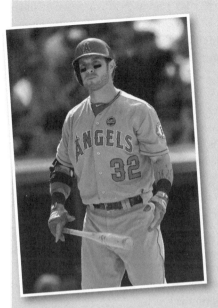

# JOSH HAMILTON

**Born:** May 21, 1981
**Height:** 6' 4"
**Weight:** 240 pounds
**Throws:** Left
**Bats:** Left

**Quote:** "One thing I can't live without is, obviously, Jesus. When I don't put Him first, my decisions don't work out too well for me. Could I have reached people being that clean-cut kid coming out of high school? Probably so. How many more people can I reach having tattoos, having an addiction problem? I've been through that . . . and I've come back."

## MAJOR LEAGUE RECORD

*Drafted:* 1st round (1st overall) by Tampa Bay Devil Rays, 1999

*MLB debut:* April 2, 2007 (age 25), with Cincinnati Reds

*Stat highlights:* 130 RBIs (2008), .359 batting average, 40 doubles (2010), 43 home runs (2012)

Nick Altrock earned baseball notoriety for a number of reasons. Consider these:

Over three years, beginning in 1904, the Cincinnati-born southpaw won 62 games for the White Sox, helping his team win the first (and so far only) all-Chicago World Series in '06. Altrock pitched for sixteen major league seasons and coached for *forty-two*. As a Washington coach, he would occasionally pinch hit for the Senators, taking his last major league swing in 1933 at age fifty-seven. According to the website baseball-reference.com, Altrock is one of only six major leaguers to play after age fifty (the others: Satchel Paige, Minnie Minoso, Jim O'Rourke, Charley O'Leary, and Jack Quinn). Altrock and Minoso are the only two players to appear in major league games in five decades.

**MAKING A SPECTACLE**

Known as a baseball comedian, Altrock often clowned in the coach's box to distract opposing pitchers. His "one man wrestling match" was said to amuse even American League president Ban Johnson—but in the interest of the game, he ordered Altrock to quit the spectacle.

The Bible's Paul once wrote that he and his fellow apostles had become a "spectacle to the whole universe" (1 Corinthians 4:9)—but it wasn't in fun. Dedicated followers of Jesus, Paul and company had given up their homes, their comfort, and their dignity to spread the Gospel message, becoming in essence, "fools for Christ" (1 Corinthians 4:10).

In a culture that's increasingly hostile to the Christian faith, we may earn a similar notoriety. But that's okay—being a spectacle in the world's eyes makes you a hero in God's.

*Sometimes you were publicly exposed to insult and persecution; at other times you stood side by side with those who were so treated. You suffered along with those in prison and joyfully accepted the confiscation of your property, because you knew that you yourselves had better and lasting possessions.*

HEBREWS 10:33–34

No less a baseball authority than Ted Williams declared, "They invented the All-Star Game for Willie Mays."

Williams had the credentials to make such a statement. An eighteen-time All-Star himself, "Player of the Decade" for the 1950s, and the twentieth century's last hitter to bat over .400 for a season, "The Splendid Splinter" saw something special in the Say Hey Kid.

## HAVING IT ALL

Rookie of the Year in 1951, Mays patrolled center field for the Giants—first in New York and then in San Francisco—for most of his twenty-two-year career. According to his Hall of Fame plaque, Mays was "one of baseball's most colorful and exciting stars," who "excelled in all phases of the game." At the time of his 1979 induction, Mays was third all-time in home runs (660), runs scored (2,062), and total bases (6,066); seventh in hits (3,283) and runs batted in (1,903); and first in putouts by an outfielder (7,095). A two-time MVP (1954 and 1965), 12-time Gold Glover, and one-time batting champion, Mays appeared in a record twenty-four All-Star games. As a player, he truly had it all.

In the non–baseball world, we use that phrase to describe a life of money and things and their related pleasures. But Jesus warned against focusing on those: "Watch out! Be on your guard against all kinds of greed; life does not consist in an abundance of possessions" (Luke 12:15).

Only in Jesus can you truly "have it all."

*I pray that you, being rooted and established in love, may have power, together with all the Lord's holy people, to grasp how wide and long and high and deep is the love of Christ, and to know this love that surpasses knowledge—that you may be filled to the measure of all the fullness of God.*
EPHESIANS 3:17–19

Baseball statistics don't reflect the emotional state of players. But details of the July 21, 1975, game between the Mets and Astros makes one wonder if Felix Millan was ticked.

**ERASED**

The New York second baseman was enjoying a productive day at the plate against Houston pitcher Ken Forsch. Millan, in the tenth of his twelve major league seasons, had slapped four consecutive singles off the 6-foot, 4-inch right-hander. But first base was as far as Millan would go on those hits.

Millan was erased each time when teammate Joe Torre, batting next in the lineup, grounded into four straight double plays. A nine-time All-Star and future New York Yankees manager, Torre just couldn't touch Forsch. In the sixteenth season of a solid eighteen-year career (he led the National League in 1971 with a .363 average and batted .297 lifetime), Torre tied a major league record for hitting futility.

Felix Millan undoubtedly hoped for more from Joe Torre that day. But it's a fact of life that people will occasionally let us down. How should we respond to such disappointments?

Jesus prescribed forgiveness, and lots of it: "If your brother or sister sins against you, rebuke them; and if they repent, forgive them. Even if they sin against you seven times in a day and seven times come back to you saying 'I repent,' you must forgive them" (Luke 17:3–4).

It may not be easy—Jesus' disciples responded by saying, "Increase our faith!" (Luke 17:5)—but it's necessary. Erase the frustrations with forgiveness and move on.

*"When you stand praying, if you hold anything against anyone, forgive them, so that your Father in heaven may forgive you your sins."*

MARK 11:25

You need pretty good eyes to determine who's who in older baseball photos—because uniform numbers were uncommon in the early 1900s.

Some players are identified easily enough by the defensive position they're playing or by their own physical characteristics—like Babe Ruth's barrel chest and bulging stomach or Hack Wilson's almost equal height and breadth.

**BY THE NUMBERS**

But to sort out every player in a picture of a home plate celebration, for example, is quite a task.

Over time, uniform numbers came into vogue, making individual players more recognizable. In 1916 the Cleveland Indians became the first team of the twentieth century to put numbers on their sleeves, though that lasted only one game. Thirteen years later, the Indians and the New York Yankees attached numbers to their uniforms permanently, and two years after that, in 1931, the American League ordered all of its teams to number their clothing.

"Identification" is a good thing in baseball, and even more so in the body of Christ. There should be something about Christians that distinguishes us from the rest of the world—something that makes it very clear just who we are. The apostle Peter suggested some good reference points: "Make every effort to add to your faith goodness; and to goodness, knowledge; and to knowledge, self-control; and to self-control, perseverance; and to perseverance, godliness; and to godliness, mutual affection; and to mutual affection, love" (2 Peter 1:5–7).

The keystone of the list is love, that valuable commodity the world seems always to long for but always to lack. When you show real love, you'll be recognized—even from the farthest seats in the bleachers.

*"By this everyone will know that you are*
*my disciples, if you love one another."*
JOHN 13:35

In 2007 some of the Colorado Rockies' best action took place off the field.

The Rocks certainly boasted some game-related highlights in '07: There was rookie shortstop Troy Tulowitzki turning the major league's thirteenth

**BEYOND THE GAME**

unassisted triple play on April 29, and the team as a whole made an amazing late-season push to reach the playoffs. Colorado won 13 of its final 14 games to force a one-game wild card tiebreaker with San Diego, winning that game 9–8 after scoring three runs in the bottom of the thirteenth inning. Marching into the postseason, the Rockies won their first-ever playoff series, steamrolling the Phillies three games to none.

But away from the cheering crowds and television cameras, Rockies players turned in a classic performance just ahead of their National League Division Series sweep. They voted to include Amanda Coolbaugh and her two young sons in Colorado's postseason financial take.

Who was Amanda Coolbaugh? She was the widow of former big-leaguer Mike Coolbaugh, a coach in the Rockies' minor league organization who was killed by a screaming line drive while coaching first base on July 22. Colorado players voted a full playoff share—potentially worth hundreds of thousands of dollars—to the grieving young family.

Widows and orphans hold a special place in God's heart, too. Several times in the Old Testament, God reminded the ancient Jews of His concern for the powerless—and urged His people to follow suit: "Learn to do right; seek justice. Defend the oppressed. Take up the cause of the fatherless; plead the case of the widow" (Isaiah 1:17).

Some things go way beyond the game of baseball. Will you?

> *Religion that God our Father accepts as pure and faultless*
> *is this: to look after orphans and widows in their distress*
> *and to keep oneself from being polluted by the world.*
> JAMES 1:27

It happens once a year for every major league team. It's traditionally attended by presidents. It fuels the dreams of hundreds of players and millions of fans.

"It" is Opening Day, the annual celebration of baseball, springtime, and hope. No matter how the last season ended, on Opening Day every team is equal—and in control of its own destiny.

**OPENING DAY**

Opening Day 2002 promised a shot at redemption for the Seattle Mariners, who won a league-record 116 games the season before but failed to reach the World Series. Opening Day 1973 gave the Boston Red Sox a chance to forget the razor-thin margin by which they missed the 1972 American League East pennant—a half game, due to contests lost in the first-ever players' strike. Opening Day 1963 meant an opportunity for the New York Mets to erase the embarrassment of their inaugural season, which lurched its way to a 40–120 finish.

Hall of Famer Lou Boudreau, the long-time Cleveland player-manager, philosophized that on Opening Day the world is all future—there is no past.

In baseball the happy dreams of Opening Day can turn into a sad reality with a single swing of an opponent's bat. But for us as Christians, there are renewal and hope in Christ that never disappoint. "If anyone is in Christ," the apostle Paul wrote to believers in Corinth, "the new creation has come: The old has gone, the new is here!" (2 Corinthians 5:17).

In Christ, every day can be "Opening Day"—a time of opportunity, hope, and joy. Take advantage of today!

*Because of the Lord's great love we are not consumed,*
*for his compassions never fail. They are new every morning;*
*great is your faithfulness.*
Lamentations 3:22-23

The term "fair" is integral to baseball: It describes the territory of the field itself, where the game progresses. If a batted ball lands in fair territory, the play continues. If a batted ball lands outside the foul lines—"not fair"—the play is dead.

**NOT FAIR!**

But longsuffering Cleveland Indians fans (who can count this author among their numbers) came out of the 2013 season muttering "not fair" in another sense.

In winning 10 straight games to conclude the regular schedule, manager Terry Francona's Tribe leapfrogged Tampa Bay and Texas for a wildcard playoff spot. In previous years, the wildcard—the team with the next-best record after the divisional winners—was guaranteed a best-of-five playoff series. But in 2013, the second year of an expanded playoff with two wildcard teams, Cleveland had to "play in," to borrow a phrase from the NCAA basketball tournament. After their long, emotional winning streak, the Indians came out flat against Tampa Bay, losing the winner-take-all wildcard game 4–0. For Tribe fans, the new rules hardly seemed fair.

Humans are all about fairness, at least as we want to define it for ourselves. But we can be thankful that God doesn't focus on what's fair—He treats His children with mercy rather than strict rules: "The LORD is compassionate and gracious, slow to anger, abounding in love. He will not always accuse, nor will he harbor his anger forever; he does not treat us as our sins deserve or repay us according to our iniquities" (Psalm 103:8–10).

Baseball fans can debate the fairness of the winner-take-all wildcard. But in the spiritual realm, "fairness" is overrated . . . what you really want is mercy.

> *"Let the wicked forsake his way and the evil man his thoughts.*
> *Let him turn to the LORD, and he will have mercy on him,*
> *and to our God, for he will freely pardon."*
> ISAIAH 54:7

Nearly two decades would pass before Johnny Cooney hit his first major league home run.

As a rookie with the 1921 Boston Braves, Cooney pitched in eight games, posting an 0–1 record and 3.92 earned run average in 20.2 innings. The 5-foot, 10-inch southpaw batted right-handed, slapping a single in five at bats.

## WHAT TOOK YOU SO LONG?

Before long, Cooney was splitting field duties among the pitcher's mound, first base, and the outfield. He notched as many as 14 wins in 1925 and achieved a batting average of .379 in 1923—though he only had 66 at bats that year.

Cooney played for the Braves until 1930, never appearing in more than 64 games in a season. After four years away from the game, he became a regular outfielder for the Brooklyn Dodgers in 1935, turning in league-leading fielding averages of .994 in 1936 and .996 five years later. But it was in 1939 that Johnny Cooney's bat finally came to life: More than eighteen years after his major league debut, he hit his first home run on September 24. Amazingly, he hit another the next day—accounting for all the home runs of his twenty-year career.

No one can say why it took Johnny Cooney so long to reach the fences. It probably wasn't procrastination—though we may need to deal with that in our own lives. If we have a tendency to put things off—even to be lazy—the Bible is clear: Get to work! "A little sleep, a little slumber, a little folding of the hands to rest—and poverty will come on you like a thief and scarcity like an armed man" (Proverbs 24:33–34).

Get to work and God is pleased—and you'll never have to hear someone say, "What took you so long?"

*Lazy hands make for poverty,*
*but diligent hands bring wealth.*
PROVERBS 10:4

As forgettable as the Atlanta Braves' strike-shortened 1981 season was, their 1982 campaign was memorable.

After finishing with 50 wins, 56 losses, and a tie in 1981, 15 games out of first place in the National League West, the Braves started 1982 on fire. They swept a two-game, season-opening series in San Diego then returned home to take three of three from the visiting Houston Astros. The home-standing Cincinnati Reds were the Braves' next victims, as Atlanta rolled on to victories six through eight.

**REBORN**

But they weren't done yet. In Houston for a second series with the Astros, Bob Horner, Dale Murphy, Chris Chambliss, and the rest of the Braves prevailed 5–3, 2–1, and 6–5 to rack up their fourth consecutive series sweep. Atlanta would then take the first two games of a three-game home set with Cincinnati before the Reds finally stopped the Braves 2–1. The thirteen-game, season-opening victory skein set a major league record and must have had many Braves fans thinking their previous year's team had been reborn.

Haven't we all wished for a fresh start, a victory string, a turnaround from previous mediocrity? That's exactly what Jesus offers, as He once told a religious leader named Nicodemus: "Flesh gives birth to flesh, but the Spirit gives birth to spirit. You should not be surprised at my saying, 'You must be born again' " (John 3:6–7).

Jesus didn't command any "religious" duties like attending church, giving money, or even being nice. Spiritual rebirth was an inner thing that came through believing in Jesus (see John 3:16).

Then, and only then, are you truly reborn—and for much longer than thirteen games.

> *Neither circumcision nor uncircumcision means*
> *anything; what counts is the new creation.*
> GALATIANS 6:15

Home runs are a hazard of the job for pitchers. Some have found the "gopher ball" more hazardous than others.

According to baseball-almanac.com, the St. Louis Cardinal's Charlie Sweeney holds the all-time record for most home runs allowed in a single game, with seven in a June 1886 contest. Four American League pitchers have allowed six dingers in a game: Tommy Thomas of St. Louis (1936), George Caster of Philadelphia (1940), Tim Wakefield of Boston (2004), and R.A. Dickey of Texas (2006).

**SERVE 'EM UP**

Minnesota's Bert Blyleven holds the single-season record for most home runs allowed, with 50 in 1986. Houston's Jose Lima follows close behind, setting the National League high of 48 in 2000.

Some pitchers allow homers year after year. Philadelphia's Robin Roberts and Chicago's Ferguson Jenkins each led the National League in home runs allowed five times—Roberts in 1954–57 and 1960, and Jenkins in 1967–68 and 1971–73.

Long careers contribute to the lifetime records, as Roberts (nineteen years played) set the all-time mark of 505 home runs allowed. Warren Spahn (twenty-one years) follows with 434, and Frank Tanana (twenty-one years) is third with 422.

Pitchers don't like to "serve 'em up," but serving is an essential part of the Christian life. "In everything I did," the apostle Paul told church leaders in Ephesus, "I showed you that by this kind of hard work we must help the weak, remembering the words the Lord Jesus himself said: 'It is more blessed to give than to receive' " (Acts 20:35).

Why not think of a person, a church program, or a charitable organization you could serve today? There's no hazard in that.

*As we have opportunity, let us do good to all people,*
*especially to those who belong to the family of believers.*
GALATIANS 6:10

# ADRIAN GONZALEZ

**Born:** May 8, 1982
**Height:** 6' 2"
**Weight:** 225 pounds
**Throws:** Left
**Bats:** Left

**Quote:** "There is no pressure. I've said all along, people talk about pressure, but who are you trying to satisfy? If you're trying to make the writers or the front office or certain people happy, then you can put pressure on yourself. But for me, it's being good for Christ, so my statistics don't matter."

## MAJOR LEAGUE RECORD

*Drafted:* 1st round (1st overall) by Florida Marlins, 2000

*MLB debut:* August 18, 2004 (age 21), with Texas Rangers

*Stat highlights:* .304 batting average (2006), 40 home runs (2009), 117 RBIs (2011), 47 doubles (2012)

Rewriting the baseball record book must be very fulfilling. Or maybe not.

Yankees outfielder Roger Maris knew firsthand the fickle nature of success. After an MVP season in 1960—when he hit 39 homers and drove in a league-high 112 runs—Maris began a historic assault on one of baseball's most imposing records: Babe Ruth's single-season home run mark of 60.

## SATISFACTION

In the thirty-three seasons since the Bambino had set the standard, only a handful of players had come close when Jimmie Foxx in 1932 and Hank Greenberg in 1938 each hit 58. Hack Wilson, in 1930, slammed 56. But in 1961, Maris—playing in "The House That Ruth Built"—launched 61 home runs to surpass baseball's most legendary slugger.

Surprisingly, the achievement angered fans who seemed to feel Maris lacked the appropriate credentials to unseat Ruth. Some record books reminded readers that the native Minnesotan had accomplished his feat in a season eight games longer than Ruth's. Major League Baseball, due to expansion, changed the traditional 154-game season to 162 games with the 1961 season.

Of the new home run record, Maris said, "All it ever brought me was trouble."

Human achievements can be that way. Apart from God, the things we most desire can become empty and unfulfilling—even frustrating—as the writer of Ecclesiastes noted. "Whoever loves money never has enough; whoever loves wealth is never satisfied with their income," he wrote (5:10). "Everyone's toil is for their mouth," he added, "yet their appetite is never satisfied" (6:7).

But the Bible also shows where real satisfaction is found, in what Ecclesiastes calls "the conclusion of the matter." Fulfillment comes to those who "fear God and keep his commandments" (12:13).

*"Why spend money on what is not bread, and your labor on what does not satisfy? Listen, listen to me, and eat what is good, and your soul will delight in the richest of fare."*
ISAIAH 55:2

Johnny Allen had a chance at baseball immortality in 1937. When the opportunity vanished before his eyes, he was none too happy.

The right-handed pitcher from Lenoir, North Carolina, showed great talent right out of the gate. As a rookie with the 1932 Yankees, Allen went 17–4 to lead the American League in winning percentage (.810). His success continued over the next several years, as he posted records of 15–7, 5–2, 13–6, and 20–10 from 1933 and 1936. In 1937, pitching for a mediocre Cleveland club, Allen was masterful—by the final day of the season, his record stood at 15–0.

**PITCHING A FIT**

With a chance to register the first perfect season by a full-time pitcher, Allen took the mound against Detroit. He pitched well enough to win but didn't, losing 1–0. Allen's resulting .938 winning percentage led the league that year and was the best in baseball history to that point. It's still the second-best all-time, after Roy Face's 18–1 season (.947) with Pittsburgh in 1959.

But for Allen, those records mattered little. He had wanted a perfect finish and blamed his season-ending loss on one hit he felt his third baseman—the appropriately nicknamed Odell "Bad News" Hale—should have prevented. Allen was so hot that he wanted to pick a postgame fight with Hale.

Before we judge Johnny Allen too harshly, perhaps we should measure our own anger: Do we have lingering resentments in our homes? What about our relationships at work or at church? How do we respond to other drivers on the road?

God's rule is simple: "Be kind and compassionate to one another, forgiving each other, just as in Christ God forgave you" (Ephesians 4:32).

*Human anger does not produce
the righteousness that God desires.*
JAMES 1:20

Bill Veeck knew there was something special about Harold Baines.

The White Sox owner brought the twenty-one-year-old rookie to Chicago in 1980. The 6-foot, 2-inch, 195-pound right fielder appeared in 141 games for the Pale Hose, batting .255 with 13 home runs. In his sophomore season, the strike-shortened 1981, Baines upped his average to .286, adding another 10 dingers. The following year began a string of six straight with at least 20 home runs.

**SEEING THE FUTURE**

Over twenty-two big league seasons—with the White Sox, Rangers, A's, Orioles, and Indians—Baines led the loop in an offensive category only once with a .541 slugging percentage in 1984. But he batted over .300 eight times, contributed to six playoff teams, and earned six All-Star selections. He finished his long career with a .289 average, 2,866 hits, and 384 home runs, the latter two totals each within the Top 50 of all time.

Just when did Veeck see Baines' great future in baseball? Pretty early—Veeck began scouting Baines in his native Maryland when he was only twelve years old.

People make their best guesses regarding what may come about, but actually seeing—and telling—the future is God's specialty. Through the prophet Isaiah, God gave details of Jesus' birth seven hundred years before it happened. And through Isaiah, He challenged other "gods" to try something similar: "Declare what is to be, present it. . . . Who foretold this long ago, who declared it from the distant past? Was it not I, the LORD? And there is no God apart from me" (Isaiah 45:21).

It's good to know that God knows everything about you—past, present, and future. And He always sees something special yet to come.

*For those God foreknew he also predestined to be*
*conformed to the image of his Son, that he might*
*be the firstborn among many brothers and sisters.*
ROMANS 8:29

For length of baseball career, it's hard to beat Connie Mack.

Born Cornelius McGillicuddy during the American Civil War, Connie Mack would enter the major leagues in 1886 with the original Washington Senators. A tall, skinny catcher—he was 6 feet, 1 inch tall and weighed about 150 pounds—Mack would play four seasons in the nation's capital, one with the Buffalo Bisons of the Player's League, and six with the Pittsburgh Pirates. He would retire from playing with an average figure of eleven years' service.

**THE LONG RUN**

There was nothing average about Mack's subsequent managerial career, though. During his final three years in Pittsburgh, Mack served as a player-manager. After a four-year hiatus from the game, he returned in 1901 to manage the brand-new Philadelphia Athletics, a charter member of the American League. The man from East Brookfield, Massachusetts, would guide the A's for their first fifty—yes, *fifty*—years. Connie Mack spent a total of sixty-one years in Major League Baseball, finally retiring at the age of eighty-eight.

*Steadfastness* and *perseverance* are biblical words that relate to a six-decade sports career. Those same words should apply to all of us as Christians. Writing to the church in Galatia, the apostle Paul encouraged believers to work long and hard at righteousness: "Let us not become weary in doing good, for at the proper time we will reap a harvest if we do not give up" (Galatians 6:9).

The long run can be tiring, but it's the way to real spiritual success. Are you as committed as Connie Mack?

> *My dear brothers and sisters, stand firm. Let nothing move you. Always give yourselves fully to the work of the Lord, because you know that your labor in the Lord is not in vain.*
> 1 CORINTHIANS 15:58

Desperate times, they say, call for desperate measures.

So in 1961, Chicago Cubs owner William Wrigley tried something new to break a string of fourteen straight second-division finishes—including five seasons in dead last. The man with the chewing gum name reinvented the role of manager by setting up a rotating "college of coaches."

## TAKE ME TO YOUR LEADER(S)

In the year that Roger Maris broke Babe Ruth's single-season home run record, the Cubs hoped that Vedie Himsl, Harry Craft, El Tappe, and Lou Klein could pool their coaching talents to create success. That, sadly, was not to be.

Himsl took the helm three separate times, piloting the club to a combined 10–21 record. Craft led twice, posting a 7–9 mark. Tappe's three opportunities produced 42 wins and 54 losses, while Klein managed a 5–6 mark in his one chance as skipper. The Cubs' overall win total of 64 was good for a seventh-place finish in the eight-team National League.

Considering the Cubs' long history of poor finishes, it's hard to pin the 1961 failure on Wrigley's unorthodox plan. But with nine managerial changes in the course of a single season, there were bound to be some problems.

Jesus once warned his disciples about a confusion of leadership: "No one can serve two masters. Either you will hate the one and love the other, or you will be devoted to the one and despise the other" (Matthew 6:24). In the context, Jesus was talking about money. But the principle applies equally to fame, power, pleasure—anything that pulls us away from God.

In the Christian life, there can be only one "manager." Only in following Him are you guaranteed a good finish.

*"Commit yourselves to the LORD and*
*serve him only, and he will deliver you."*
1 SAMUEL 7:3

For a team facing a 12-run deficit, the game is all but over. Almost always.

Three times in major league history, though, a club has come from down by a dozen to win. The Chicago White Sox were the first in 1911; fourteen years later, the Philadelphia Athletics duplicated the feat. Then seventy-six years would pass before it happened again.

**STILL IN THE GAME**

Enter the 2001 Cleveland Indians, battling for their sixth playoff spot in seven years. Hosting the red-hot Seattle Mariners, who would win a major league record 116 games that season, the Tribe found themselves trailing 12–0 after just three innings.

In the middle of the seventh, Seattle led 14–2—at which point the Indians began their historic comeback. Scoring three in the seventh, four in the eighth, and five in the ninth, Cleveland forced extra innings. In the bottom of the eleventh, utility man Jolbert Cabrera slapped a broken-bat single to score Kenny Lofton for one of the more remarkable wins in the annals of baseball.

On August 6, 2001, not even a 12-run deficit could stop the Cleveland Indians. Those of us who follow Jesus Christ can expect even greater victories.

"I am convinced," the apostle Paul wrote, "that neither death nor life, neither angels nor demons, neither the present nor the future, nor any powers, neither height nor depth, nor anything else in all creation, will be able to separate us from the love of God that is in Christ Jesus our Lord" (Romans 8:38–39).

If you're deep in the hole today, take heart. As God's child, you're always still in the game.

*We have this hope as an anchor for the soul, firm and secure.*
HEBREWS 6:19

You never know what you might see late in a baseball season.

Rookies may get their first chance to appear on a major league field, and managers may experiment with new and unusual defensive combinations. There was a little of both on September 13, 1963, when San Francisco skipper Alvin Dark briefly created an all-brother outfield of Felipe, Matty, and Jesus Alou.

## THE BROTHERS ALOU

The three Dominicans would ultimately play a combined forty-seven years in the big leagues, but on this night, twenty-one-year-old Jesus was a newly minted rookie. Middle brother Matty, age twenty-four, was in his fourth year with the Giants, while twenty-eight-year-old Felipe was in his sixth and final season with the Bay Area Nationals.

For the next two years, Felipe would wear the uniform of the Milwaukee Braves, while Matty and Jesus stayed together as Giants. In 1966 Matty joined the Pittsburgh Pirates, and the three were completely separated until 1973, when Felipe and Matty would play a partial season together as New York Yankees. But for part of the 1963 campaign, and for a few special moments of one particular game, Felipe, Matty, and Jesus Alou were all together—as brothers should be.

The writer of Hebrews once urged brothers in Christ—sisters, too—to make the effort to be together: "Let us . . . not [give] up meeting together, as some are in the habit of doing, but [encourage] one another—and all the more as you see the Day approaching" (Hebrews 10:24–25).

What better place for meeting together than church? Will you be there this Sunday?

*[Jesus] went to Nazareth, where he had been brought up, and on the Sabbath day he went into the synagogue, as was his custom.*
LUKE 4:16

Yankee pinstripes were good for Lefty Gomez, and he knew it.

The Hall of Famer pitched for New York from 1930 to 1942, piling up 189 career victories against 102 losses. In three of his thirteen seasons

## THE RIGHT UNIFORM

with the Yankees, Gomez recorded an earned run average of 2.63 or less, winning 21, 21, and 26 games. In 1932 he won 24 games, in spite of a rather hefty 4.21 ERA. Gomez once quipped, "The secret to my success is clean living and a fast outfield"—and it certainly didn't hurt that he had hitters like Babe Ruth and Lou Gehrig backing him up either.

When New York released Gomez, he moved on to Washington for the 1943 season. His career with the Senators was brief, though—Lefty started only one game, giving up four runs, three of them earned, in 4.2 innings pitched. He promptly retired from the game with a final-season record of 0–1 and an ERA of 5.79.

The right uniform was clearly an element of Lefty Gomez's success. The same goes for us as Christians. Writing to the church at Colossae, the apostle Paul commanded believers to "put to death" feelings like lust and greed (Colossians 3:5), and "rid yourselves" of things like anger and filthy language (Colossians 3:8). Then he compared our attitudes and actions to a set of clothing—a uniform, if you will—when he said, "Do not lie to each other, since you have taken off your old self with its practices and have put on the new self, which is being renewed in knowledge in the image of its Creator" (Colossians 3:9–10).

The spiritual "clothing" you wear is up to you. Which uniform will you choose today?

*All of you who were baptized into Christ have clothed yourselves with Christ.*
GALATIANS 3:27

When you really think about it, baseball's "Iron Men"—like Cal Ripken Jr., and Lou Gehrig—were just doing their jobs.

That's not meant to diminish their accomplishments. Ripken played in 2,632 consecutive games between May 29, 1982, and September 20, 1998. The Baltimore infielder's streak broke what many believed to be the untouchable

**JUST DOING MY JOB**

record of Yankee first baseman Lou Gehrig, who had gone 2,130 games without a day off from 1925 to 1939.

Only four other players in the long history of Major League Baseball have played in at least a thousand consecutive games: Everett "Deacon" Scott strung together 1,307 straight appearances with the Red Sox and Yankees in the late teens and early 1920s; the Dodgers' Steve Garvey played exactly one hundred fewer consecutive games, 1,207, in the late 1970s and early 1980s; Billy Williams appeared in 1,117 straight games for the Chicago Cubs in the mid- to late 1960s; and shortstop Joe Sewell was the Cleveland Indians' "Iron Man" through the 1920s, with 1,103 consecutive games played. Sixth on the list is Cardinals superstar Stan Musial, with 895 consecutive games played in the 1950s.

In baseball, that kind of dependability wins accolades. In the Christian life, steady regularity is a basic expectation. Jesus—defining His disciples' obligations to God—once compared them to a servant who finished his work in the field then immediately served dinner to his master. "Will [the master] thank the servant because he did what he was told to do?" Jesus asked. "So you also, when you have done everything you were told to do, should say, 'We are unworthy servants; we have only done our duty'" (Luke 17:9–10).

Don't expect a standing ovation in this life. Work for God's "Well done, good and faithful servant!" (Matthew 25:21).

*Humble yourselves before the Lord, and he will lift you up.*
JAMES 4:10

Any team could have used Dave Winfield's services. Several did.

The big outfielder, elected to the Hall of Fame in 2001, played for the San Diego Padres, New York Yankees, California Angels, Toronto Blue Jays,

**IN DEMAND**

Minnesota Twins, and Cleveland Indians over a very productive twenty-two-year career.

Though the 6-foot, 6-inch 220-pounder led the league in a major offensive category just once (with 118 RBIs in 1979), he recorded several career numbers that rank him among the Top 25 players of all time: 3,110 hits, 1,833 runs batted in, and 465 home runs. Over his major league tenure, Winfield recorded a solid .283 batting average. He was a good fielder with a strong arm, and his 223 career stolen bases attest to his speed.

Dave Winfield's athletic skills weren't limited to baseball, though. Upon leaving the University of Minnesota, he was drafted by four teams in three sports: baseball, basketball, and football. He also excelled in the classroom.

Wouldn't it be nice to be as "in demand" as Dave Winfield was? Actually, you are—by the greatest Audience of all and not for any particular skill or ability you may have. Here's how the prophet Jeremiah explained it: "The LORD appeared to us in the past, saying: 'I have loved you with an everlasting love; I have drawn you with unfailing kindness' " (Jeremiah 31:3).

"In demand" by God Himself, safe in His love that never changes— that should give you confidence, whatever may happen today.

> "No one can come to me [Jesus] unless the Father who sent
> me draws them, and I will raise them up at the last day."
> JOHN 6:44

# JEREMY AFFELDT

**Born:** June 6, 1979
**Height:** 6' 5"
**Weight:** 225 pounds
**Throws:** Left
**Bats:** Left

**Quote:** "Jesus loved on people first. He gained a voice in their lives, and when they asked for His view, he gave it to them. He didn't soapbox it right out of the gate. That's my deal with kids. I want to empower them."

## MAJOR LEAGUE RECORD

***Drafted:*** 3rd round by Kansas City Royals, 1997

***MLB debut:*** April 6, 2002 (age 22), with Kansas City Royals

***Stat highlights:*** 126 innings pitched, 98 strikeouts (2003), 13 saves (2004), 1.73 ERA (2009)

Baseball games typically consist of nine innings. But there are exceptions to that rule.

"Extra innings" occur when teams are tied after the regulation nine. Today we'll focus on shortened games, those "called" for various reasons.

**GAME CALLED BY. . .**

Most common today is the rain-shortened ball game, though in baseball's early days before lights, darkness ended many contests before the ninth. In some cases in the late nineteenth and early twentieth centuries, games were even called to allow visiting teams to catch a train home.

Of all history's called games, perhaps the strangest occurred on September 15, 1946, in Brooklyn. The Dodgers were leading the Cubs 2–0 in the sixth when a swarm of gnats invaded Ebbets Field. Brooklyn right-hander Kirby Higbe, an All-Star and 17-game winner that year, was so busy waving the bugs away that he couldn't throw a pitch. Umpires called the game, although officially they said it was for darkness.

Interestingly, both darkness and gnats were among the ten plagues God sent on Egypt prior to the Exodus. Plague number three: "When Aaron stretched out his hand with the staff and struck the dust of the ground, gnats came upon people and animals" (Exodus 8:17). Plague number nine: "Moses stretched out his hand toward the sky and total darkness covered all Egypt for three days" (Exodus 10:22).

God was convincing Pharaoh to let his slaves—the Israelites—leave Egypt to go to their promised land of Canaan. The Lord used any means at His disposal to get Pharaoh's attention and accomplish His purpose.

Does God have your attention these days?

> *"So is my word that goes out from my mouth: It will not return to me empty, but will accomplish what I desire and achieve the purpose for which I sent it."*
> ISAIAH 55:11

As dads often teach their boys baseball, it's not unusual to find cases of fathers and sons in the major leagues.

Some recent examples: Ken Griffey and Ken Jr.; Felipe Alou and Moises; Sandy Alomar Sr., Sandy Jr., and Roberto; Bob Boone, Aaron, and Bret. In each case, the sons have had respectable careers, sometimes surpassing those of their fathers. Then there's the story of Pete Rose Jr.

## FATHERS AND SONS

The younger Rose joined his dad's old team, the Reds, as a September call-up in 1997. The twenty-seven-year-old rookie, son of the man whose 3,562 games and 4,256 hits are all-time major league records, managed only a pair of singles in fourteen at bats, striking out nine times. His eleven games with the Reds would be his only big league experience.

In getting to baseball's highest level, the junior Rose likely had an advantage over other players without famous fathers, but once there his fate was in his own hands. A similar principle applies to the Christian life.

Having believing parents, attending a good church, or knowing the right people may give some of us greater spiritual opportunities—but the responsibility to accept the Gospel truth rests squarely with each individual. In the book of Jeremiah, God spoke of the "new covenant" He was planning, the Christian era when "people will no longer say, 'The parents have eaten sour grapes, and the children's teeth are set on edge.' Instead, everyone will die for their own sin" (Jeremiah 31:29–30). The flipside of that coin is Romans 10:13: "Everyone who calls on the name of the Lord will be saved."

Don't pin your hopes on anyone else's faith. What your father may have done doesn't count in Christianity.

*The child will not share the guilt of the parent, nor will the parent share the guilt of the child. The righteousness of the righteous will be credited to them, and the wickedness of the wicked will be charged against them.*
EZEKIEL 18:20

Diomedes Olivo's major league career was brief. It almost had to be, considering his late start.

The left-handed pitcher from the Dominican Republic is remembered

**OLD ROOKIE**

as one of the oldest rookies ever to play in the big leagues. Olivo was forty-one years old when he joined the Pittsburgh Pirates in 1960, appearing as a reliever in four games. He held his own with the Bucs: though he recorded no wins or losses, he gave up only eight hits in 9.2 innings, striking out 10 and posting an earned run average of 2.79.

In 1961 Olivo was out of the majors, but the Pirates brought him back again the next season. As a forty-three-year-old sophomore, he appeared in 62 games—including one start. This time around, Olivo was 5–1 with a 2.77 ERA.

He was a Cardinal in the '63 season—but in 19 games, the now forty-four-year-old was clearly slowing down. Olivo gave up nine runs in 13.1 innings, ballooning his ERA to 5.40, and he finished the season 0–5. St. Louis would be the last stop for Olivo, whose motto could have been "better late than never."

Jesus' parable of the vineyard workers (Matthew 20:1–16) described some other latecomers—people who came to the kingdom late, missing the hard work the earlier laborers had done. It was a picture of salvation, which God is pleased to give anyone at any time: "I want to give the one who was hired last the same as I gave you. Don't I have the right to do what I want with my own money? Or are you envious because I am generous?" (Matthew 20:14–15).

Whenever you became a "rookie" in the kingdom, be thankful. It's purely the gift of a generous God.

> *"So the last will be first, and the first will be last."*
> MATTHEW 20:16

Baseball history is rich in quirky characters and memorable tales. Consider the case of Dizzy Dean, hero of the 1934 World Series.

Born Jay Hanna Dean in Lucas, Arkansas, "Dizzy" became one of the great pitchers of his era. The Cardinals' right-hander won 120 games between 1932 and 1936, notching a superb 30–7 record in St. Louis' championship season.

**EMPTY-HEADED**

He was boastful but good-natured and kept his brother—fellow Cardinal hurler Paul "Daffy" Dean—laughing with his wisecracks. The duo pitched all four of St. Louis' victories in the '34 Series, and Dizzy even contributed on the base paths: as a pinch runner in Game 4, he broke up a double play attempt when the Detroit fielder's throw conked him on the head.

It was an incident that led to one of baseball's great stories. A newspaper account of the beaning and its aftermath carried the classic headline:

> DEAN'S HEAD EXAMINED,
> X-RAYS REVEAL NOTHING

Dizzy Dean wasn't really as empty-headed as those two sentences implied. But you have to wonder about the man the Bible describes in Psalm 53:1—"The fool says in his heart, 'There is no God.' "

Few of us would ever say or think that. But do we sometimes *live* as if there is no God—a kind of practical atheism? Be sure of this: God knows every thought we think, every word we say, and every deed we do. But remember this, too: He loved us enough to send His Son, Jesus, to die on the cross for our sins.

Who wants to be a fool? Fill your head with thoughts of God.

*And he said to the human race, "The fear of the Lord—*
*that is wisdom, and to shun evil is understanding."*
JOB 28:28

For a hitter, there's no thrill quite like a late inning, game-changing home run. Unless, that is, the shot is called back.

On July 24, 1983, Kansas City superstar George Brett was riding high

**PICKY, PICKY**

after hitting a two-out, two-run homer in Yankee Stadium. The future Hall of Famer's blast changed a 4–3 ninth inning deficit into a 5–4 Royals lead.

The joy soon faded, though, when New York manager Billy Martin asked home plate umpire Tim McClelland to inspect Brett's bat. Earlier in the season, Yankee third baseman Graig Nettles had noticed that Brett seemed to use more pine tar than the rules allowed—and Martin had saved that choice information for just such a moment as this.

McClelland measured the goo on Brett's bat, finding it exceeded the eighteen inches allowed. Brett was called out, erasing the home run and giving the Yankees a 4–3 victory. The Royals were incensed by the ruling, which was later overturned by American League president Lee McPhail, who said "games should be won and lost on the playing field—not through technicalities of the rules."

Baseball's official acknowledgment of the "bigger picture" is reminiscent of Jesus' approach to God's laws. Arguing with hypocritical Pharisees, Jesus once said, "You give a tenth of your spices—mint, dill and cumin. But you have neglected the more important matters of the law—justice, mercy and faithfulness. You should have practiced the latter, without neglecting the former" (Matthew 23:23). Our concern for the letter of the law should be balanced by an equal concern for the spirit of the law.

If you're inclined to spiritual pickiness, don't forget the "more important matters."

> He has shown you, O mortal, what is good. And what
> does the LORD require of you? To act justly and to
> love mercy and to walk humbly with your God.
> MICAH 6:8

Any list of baseball's most memorable moments would have to include Eddie Gaedel's one-and-done plate appearance for the St. Louis Browns.

On August 19, 1951, in a game against the Detroit Tigers, Gaedel strode to the batter's box as a pinch hitter. Actually, "strode" might be overstating things a bit since Gaedel was on the short side—he was just over three and a half feet tall.

## PLAYING "SHORT"

The man who in less sensitive times was known as a midget, wearing the number "⅛" on the back of his tiny uniform, had been enlisted by Browns owner Bill Veeck Jr. to get a base on balls. Gaedel found success—his strike zone was so small that Detroit hurler Bob Cain missed on four straight pitches.

Veeck, who as the Indians' owner had made Satchel Paige a forty-two-year-old "rookie" and who later would unveil an exploding scoreboard at Chicago's Comiskey Park, was well-known for his publicity-oriented stunts. Gaedel's at bat, though it did give the Browns a base runner, was also a good joke, one that's still funny more than sixty years after it happened.

Those who believe God has a sense of humor point to the fact that humans, made in His image, like to laugh. And when Jesus promised His followers joy, it seems logical that mirth would be a part of that. But as with so many aspects of life, the Bible offers a word of warning, too: "Nor should there be obscenity, foolish talk or coarse joking, which are out of place, but rather thanksgiving" (Ephesians 5:4).

A good laugh can make any situation better. Just make sure that it's truly a *good* laugh.

*Sin is not ended by multiplying words,*
*but the prudent hold their tongues.*
PROVERBS 10:19

Ted Williams had one overriding baseball ambition: to be the greatest hitter who ever lived. Though the phrase "greatest hitter" leaves room for debate, the Red Sox slugger certainly accomplished amazing things with his bat.

**RISKING .400**

His career average of .344 ties him for sixth place all-time, behind Ty Cobb (.366), Rogers Hornsby (.358), Joe Jackson (.356), Ed Delahanty (.346), and Tris Speaker (.345). But Williams hit for power as well as average. His career home run total of 521, in the Top 15 all-time, ranges from 220 more than Hornsby's to 467 more than Jackson's.

In 1941 Williams became the last player of the twentieth century to bat over .400 for an entire season. On the final day of the campaign, with a double header on the schedule, the "Splendid Splinter's" batting average was .3995. Rounded up, it would have qualified as the major leagues' first .400 season in seventeen years. Still, Williams played both games that day—and his six-for-eight performance boosted his season-ending average to .406. It was a risky move, putting his .400 batting on the line, but it paid off handsomely.

The stakes were much higher for three Bible characters who literally risked their lives on God's faithfulness. Hananiah, Mishael, and Azariah—better known as Shadrach, Meshach, and Abednego—refused to bow to King Nebuchadnezzar's image of gold and earned themselves a visit to the "fiery furnace." Nearly anyone who's ever been to Sunday school knows how the story ends: In the king's words, "Praise be to the God of Shadrach, Meshach and Abednego, who has sent his angel and rescued his servants!" (Daniel 3:28).

In human terms, theirs was a dangerous move, too—but ultimately, for Christians, it's never risky to obey God.

*The LORD will watch over your coming and going both now and forevermore.*
PSALM 121:8

We rightfully celebrate those few pitchers who've thrown perfect games. But the guys on the other side make an interesting study, too.

For every perfect-game hurler, at least nine opposing batters tried manfully—but unsuccessfully—to break up the gem. Today, let's consider just one, Joey Amalfitano, and his appearance in Sandy Koufax's September 9, 1965, perfecto in Los Angeles.

**SOUNDS LIKE A BALL**

The Cubs' middle infielder was called to pinch hit with one out in the ninth. Amalfitano stepped to the plate to face a pitcher who had set down twenty-five in a row, the four most recent by strikeout. On just three pitches, Amalfitano became the fifth straight victim of the K.

Koufax had such good stuff that the Cub batter quipped to home plate umpire Ed Vargo that the first pitch, a called fastball, "sounded high." We're left to assume he never saw it coming.

Isn't that like life? Many times events and experiences blow past us—and we're left to guess at what exactly happened. But God knows with a big-picture view that Job described: "Does he not see my ways and count my every step?" (Job 31:4).

For some, that's frightening. They see God as an Orwellian "Big Brother" just waiting to catch them doing wrong—and then punish them for it.

But God is love (1 John 4:8) and takes "no pleasure in the death of anyone" (Ezekiel 18:32). His complete knowledge of who we are, what we think, and what we do can really be comforting. God knows exactly what's happening, even when you can't see what life is throwing at us.

*"Who can hide in secret places so that I cannot see them?"*
*declares the LORD. "Do I not fill heaven and earth?"*
JEREMIAH 23:24

Today, let's test your baseball knowledge:

What do Dave Bancroft, Bill Dahlen, Tommy Corcoran, Rabbit Maranville, and Luke Appling have in common?

**THROWS RIGHT**

If we add Luis Aparicio, Larry Bowa, Dave Concepcion, Ozzie Smith, and Cal Ripken Jr. to the list, does the common thread become more obvious?

Each played shortstop—in fact, they're the major leagues' Top 10 all-time assist leaders for the position. Their careers spanned more than a century, from 1890 to 2001. They came from places like Massachusetts, Iowa, California, and Venezuela. Most were of average size, though Ripken (6 feet, 4 inches, 225 pounds) and Maranville (5 feet, 5 inches, 155 pounds) stand out as exceptions.

One characteristic each man shared was a good throwing arm—in every case, his right. Right-handedness is essentially a prerequisite for shortstops, not to mention second and third basemen. The last major league regular to buck the convention, throwing left-handed from one of those three positions, was Philadelphia Phillies shortstop Billy Hulen, way back in 1896.

When applying for certain baseball positions, "right" is the operative word. It's an awfully important term in the Christian life, too.

"Be careful to do what is right in the eyes of everyone," the apostle Paul wrote to the church in Rome. One way to do that: "Do not repay anyone evil for evil." Another: "If it is possible, as far as it depends on you, live at peace with everyone" (Romans 12:17–18).

In the Christian realm, right makes might. What right can you do today?

> *"If you do what is right, will you not be accepted? But if you do not do what is right, sin is crouching at your door."*
> GENESIS 4:7

There are great catches, and then there's "The Catch."

It happened in Game 1 of the 1954 World Series between the New York Giants and Cleveland Indians. After winning an American League record 111 games, the Tribe was poised to take the early advantage in the Fall Classic. With the score tied at two in the eighth, two runners on, Cleveland first baseman Vic

**THE CATCH**

Wertz smashed a shot toward the Polo Grounds' spacious center field. But what Indian fans hoped would be a bases-clearing double or triple became simply a long out when New York star Willie Mays made one of the most remarkable catches in Major League history.

The third-year center fielder turned and sprinted directly away from Wertz, snaring the ball in an over-the-shoulder shocker some 450 feet from home plate. Mays' heroics stifled the Cleveland rally, allowing New York to win the game in extra innings and the series in a four-game sweep. More than a half century later, fans are still moved by black-and-white footage of "The Catch."

Another amazing catch is found in the Bible's book of John. This catch, of fish, happened on the Sea of Galilee shortly after Jesus' resurrection. Seeing several disciples on a boat, Jesus called out from shore, "Friends, haven't you any fish?" (John 21:5). When they answered no, Jesus replied, " 'Throw your net on the right side of the boat and you will find some.' When they did, they were unable to haul the net in because of the large number of fish" (John 21:6).

The miraculous catch assured the disciples that Jesus was alive—and gave them a morning meal. Two thousand years later, Jesus is still alive, and He's still meeting the needs of His people.

*My God will meet all your needs according*
*to the riches of his glory in Christ Jesus.*
PHILIPPIANS 4:19

# STEPHEN DREW

**Born:** March 16, 1983
**Height:** 6'
**Weight:** 190 pounds
**Throws:** Right
**Bats:** Left

**Quote:** "Things don't always go your way. People sometimes get a wrong perspective of Christians—like it's always easy. It can be the total opposite. But with Jesus sitting there with you, He can hold your hand through things. He's there with you. You might not be able to see it now, but you can look back and see He's got His hand on you the whole time."

## MAJOR LEAGUE RECORD

*Drafted:* 1st round (15th overall) by Arizona Diamondbacks, 2004

*MLB debut:* July 15, 2006 (age 23), with Arizona Diamondbacks

*Stat highlights:* .21 home runs, 44 doubles, 67 RBIs (2008), 12 triples (2009, 2010)

Change, we are told, is inevitable. Just ask the Montreal Expos.

Major League Baseball went international in 1969 when the Expos joined the new Eastern Division of the National League. Managed by veteran skipper Gene Mauch, the Montreal contingent featured a young right fielder named Rusty Staub and an old reliever, Roy Face, in his final year in the majors.

**TRANSFORMED**

As is often the case with expansion teams, the Expos struggled—finishing 52–110.

A second-division squad for its first decade, Montreal reeled off three straight runner-up finishes between 1979 and 1981. The Expos would never top their division until 1994—though, in a cruel twist of fate, a players' strike caused the cancellation of the World Series that year.

More bad luck followed as the Expos' financial problems caused the twenty-nine other major league teams to purchase the club in 2002. By 2005 they were no longer even the Montreal Expos—they had transformed into the Washington Nationals.

Transformation of a far greater sort awaits us as Christians. After a lifetime of hard work, sickness, aches, and pains—and, ultimately, death—we can each look forward to a sleek new body that will operate perfectly and last forever. "We know that if the earthly tent we live in is destroyed," the apostle Paul wrote, "we have a building from God, an eternal house in heaven, not built by human hands" (2 Corinthians 5:1).

God loves to change people for the better—transforming not only your heart and mind, but ultimately your body, too.

*Listen, I tell you a mystery: We will not all sleep, but we will all be changed—in a flash, in the twinkling of an eye, at the last trumpet. For the trumpet will sound, the dead will be raised imperishable, and we will be changed.*

1 CORINTHIANS 15:51–52

Imagine this: You're a major league pitcher working on a perfect game. After six innings, not a single opponent has reached base. Same thing after seven innings, and then eight. The excitement builds as you continue your masterful performance. In the ninth, you mow down the opposition one-two-three—perfection!

**ALMOST PERFECT**

Well, kind of. You see, your team hasn't scored, so you're going to extra innings.

In the tenth, eleventh, and twelfth innings you continue to baffle batters and remain perfect after thirty-six outs. But still your offense hasn't supported you. In the thirteenth, your defense fails you—an error allows a runner on base. After an intentional walk, the next batter doubles home the one run that ruins your stunning effort.

Sound like a nightmare? It actually happened to Pittsburgh's Harvey Haddix on May 26, 1959, against the Milwaukee Braves.

That crushing end to a truly magical performance begs a parallel to the life of the biblical King David. The "man after God's own heart" wasted a lifetime of obedience by yielding to a single passionate desire: "One evening David got up from his bed and walked around on the roof of the palace. From the roof he saw a woman bathing. The woman was very beautiful. . . . Then David sent messengers to get her. She came to him, and he slept with her" (2 Samuel 11:2, 4).

If David's adultery with Bathsheba wasn't bad enough, he compounded the problem by having her husband, Uriah, killed. Who would have expected such a late-inning disaster in the king's life?

"Almost perfect" was still a loss for Harvey Haddix. It was a far more serious defeat for King David.

*Flee the evil desires of youth, and pursue righteousness, faith, love and peace, along with those who call on the Lord out of a pure heart.*
2 TIMOTHY 2:22

Americans love a good rags-to-riches, "pull yourself up by your bootstraps" story. Like that of Wade Boggs.

The Omaha, Nebraska, native accomplished so much in his eighteen-year big league career that it's easy to forget his humble beginnings. The future superstar of the Boston Red Sox, New York Yankees, and Tampa Bay Devil Rays was **BOAST WORTHY** selected in the seventh round of the 1976 draft, the 166th player chosen overall.

It was a rather inauspicious start, followed by six years in the minor leagues. But with Boston in 1982, Boggs hit the ground running, batting .349 in 104 games. In his sophomore season, he posted a league-leading .361 batting average then topped the circuit for four straight years, 1985–88, with figures of .368, .357, .363, and .366. Boggs was the only player of the twentieth century to notch at least 200 hits in seven straight seasons (1983–89), including a league-leading 240 in '85. He retired after the 1999 season with an overall batting average of .328 and was elected to the Hall of Fame in his first year of eligibility.

In the business world, men who make such a climb are said to be "self-made" and often share their "secrets of success" in books, magazines, and television interviews. It would be hard not to be proud of such accomplishments.

But Christians don't have the luxury of basking in their achievements. Through the prophet Jeremiah, God Himself said, "Let not the wise boast of their wisdom or the strong boast of their strength or the rich boast of their riches, but let the one who boasts boast about this: that they have the understanding to know me" (Jeremiah 9:23–24).

Ultimately, your relationship to God is all that matters.

*May I never boast except in the cross of our Lord Jesus Christ, through which the world has been crucified to me, and I to the world.*
GALATIANS 6:14

In one corner, Goliath—the Oakland A's. In the other, looking puny in comparison, David—also known as the Cincinnati Reds.

The 1990 World Series had the look of a complete mismatch. Oakland,

## DAVID AND GOLIATH

the reigning champions of baseball, were in the series for the third straight year, boasting the likes of Mark McGwire (39 home runs, 108 runs batted in), Jose Canseco (37 home runs, 101 RBIs), and Rickey Henderson (28 home runs, 65 steals). On the mound, the A's featured 27-game winner Bob Welch (2.95 ERA), 22-game winner Dave Stewart (2.56), and closer Dennis Eckersley, who saved 48 games with an astounding 0.61 ERA. The A's had rolled into the postseason with 103 wins, four more than in 1989 when they swept the "earthquake series" from the San Francisco Giants.

The Reds, on the other hand, notched 91 victories with an ensemble cast of players like Barry Larkin, Eric Davis, and Paul O'Neill. The Redlegs were playing their first World Series since the Big Red Machine teams of the mid-1970s.

As many expected, the series was a blowout. What few expected was that the Reds would dispatch the A's in four games. David had clearly conquered Goliath.

Who knows what caused Cincinnati's stunning upset of Oakland? In the original David and Goliath story, though, the power behind the little guy's victory was clear: "The Lord who rescued me from the paw of the lion and the paw of the bear will rescue me from the hand of this Philistine" (1 Samuel 17:37).

Facing a Goliath today? In God's power, you can win big.

> Some trust in chariots and some in horses,
> but we trust in the name of the Lord our God.
> Psalm 20:7

When the on-field competition has ended, baseball's postseason awards provide a final touch of suspense for a given year. Who will be rookie or manager or comeback player of the year? Which fielders will receive Gold Gloves?

The major leagues' biggest honor, Most Valuable Player, began in 1911 as the Chalmers Award. Sponsored by an **HONORED** automobile manufacturer, it was intended to celebrate the "most important and useful player to his club and to the league." The initial award in the National League went to the Cubs' Frank "Wildfire" Schulte, who batted an even .300 and led the loop with 21 home runs and 107 RBIs.

In the American League, the unanimous choice was Ty Cobb with an avalanche of league-leading stats: a glittering .420 batting average on 248 hits, including 47 doubles and 24 triples; 147 runs scored and another 127 driven in; a slugging average of .621; and 83 stolen bases.

In 1956 pitchers got their own award, created to honor all-time win leader Cy Young, who had died the previous year. Brooklyn's Don Newcombe, with league-leading totals in wins (27) and winning percentage (.794), took home the first trophy.

Honors are fun—and we as Christians can look forward to some heavenly recognition. But not the competitive, winner-takes-all kind. "My Father will honor the one who serves me," Jesus said. "Whoever serves me must follow me; and where I am, my servant also will be" (John 12:26).

God's awards are for humble, obedient, consistent service. And every one of us has the potential to win.

*For the LORD God is a sun and shield; the LORD bestows favor and honor; no good thing does he withhold from those whose walk is blameless.*
PSALM 84:11

Dave Kingman hit a bunch of home runs—but not a lot else.

The 6-foot, 6-inch slugger played sixteen major league seasons for the San Francisco Giants, New York Mets, San Diego Padres, California

**KING KONG**

Angels, New York Yankees, Chicago Cubs, and Oakland A's. During that time, 1971 through 1986, the man nicknamed "Kong" belted 442 home runs, putting him around the Top 30 of all time.

But Kingman recorded only 1,575 hits in his career, yielding a rather lackluster batting average of .236. The big man from Pendleton, Oregon, had his best year at the plate in 1979, when he hit .288 for the Cubs, leading the league with 48 round trippers. Three years later, with the Mets, Kingman again led the league in home runs (37) but hit a meager .204. That set a major league record for the lowest batting average by a home run leader.

Dave Kingman was a notable mixture of strengths and weaknesses. There are several parallels in the Bible—including the example of the apostle Paul.

The great missionary and church leader wrote almost half of the books of the New Testament, performed miracles, even got a guided tour of heaven. But he wrote to fellow believers in Rome (in what we now know as Romans chapter 7) that he struggled to do the right thing. Always feeling an internal tug-of-war between godliness and temptation, Paul wrote, "I myself in my mind am a slave to God's law, but in the sinful nature a slave to the law of sin" (Romans 7:25).

If spiritual consistency is a challenge for you, too, take heart in the example of Paul. Just keep looking to God to bring you through.

> *No temptation has overtaken you except what is common to mankind. And God is faithful; he will not let you be tempted beyond what you can bear. But when you are tempted, he will also provide a way out so that you can endure it.*
> 1 CORINTHIANS 10:13

You might need a scorecard to keep track of major league team names through history. Case in point, Cleveland's.

In the late 1800s, when the major leagues were beginning to form, the northeast Ohio city boasted the National League Blues for six seasons, the Players League Infants for a single year, and the Spiders, who spent two seasons in the

**NAME GAME**

American Association before jumping ship to the National League for a decade. Ultimately, all three teams went out of business.

When the American League formed in 1901, Cleveland was among the eight cities fielding a club—but not immediately as the Indians. Fans cheered for the Blues that first year then for the Bronchos in 1902, the Naps (for their player/manager Nap Lajoie) from 1903 to 1909, and even for the Molly McGuires from 1910 to 1914. The "Indians" name came about by fan vote in 1915.

What's in a name? In baseball, some interesting historical footnotes. In our individual lives, a reminder of what God has done for us through Jesus Christ. In his first letter to the Corinthians, the apostle Paul presented a list of very undesirable names—including "sexually immoral," "idolators," "thieves," "swindlers," and "drunkards"—going on to say, "And that is what some of you *were*" (1 Corinthians 6:11, emphasis added). There's more good news in the second part of the verse: "But you were washed, you were sanctified, you were justified in the name of the Lord Jesus Christ and by the Spirit of our God."

We can thank God that all those bad names that once described us are history—just like all the odd monikers that predate "Indians."

*"The one who is victorious I will make a pillar in the temple of my God. . . . I will also write on them my new name."*
REVELATION 3:12

"Eventful" well describes baseball's 1998 season.

The thrilling home run chase between Mark McGwire and Sammy Sosa (sadly, we now know it was fueled by performance-enhancing drugs) happened in 1998. So did the record-tying 20-strikeout performance by Cubs' rookie Kerry Wood—in just his fifth major league start. The Yankees won a new American League record 114 games, and the majors welcomed two more expansion clubs—in Tampa Bay and Arizona.

**SWAPPING ALLEGIANCE**

And then there was the case of the Milwaukee Brewers. The team that began as the Seattle Pilots in 1969, moving to the land of brats and beer the following season, became the first and only major league team of the twentieth century to change leagues. The Brewers agreed to switch from the American League to the National so the two new teams, the Devil Rays and Diamondbacks, could play in separate associations. After twenty-eight years as an American League team, Milwaukee swapped its allegiance.

When we accept Christ, we, too, swap our allegiance—from the sin and selfishness that characterize our natural human existence to the completely countercultural life of God's Spirit. As the apostle Paul wrote, "For the grace of God has appeared that offers salvation to all people. It teaches us to say 'No' to ungodliness and worldly passions, and to live self-controlled, upright and godly lives in this present age" (Titus 2:11–12).

Have you truly made the switch?

*Don't you know that when you offer yourselves to someone as obedient slaves, you are slaves of the one you obey—whether you are slaves to sin, which leads to death, or to obedience, which leads to righteousness?*
ROMANS 6:16

Even casual fans of the game know that *AL* stands for American League, the "junior circuit" that began in 1901 to compete with the well-established National League.

Add an *S* to those initials, though, and you have something else entirely. ALS is **LOU GEHRIG'S DISEASE** amyotrophic lateral sclerosis, commonly known as Lou Gehrig's disease, the neurological disorder that caused the Yankee star's premature death at age thirty-seven.

Until his health failed him, "Larrupin' Lou" was one of the game's greatest players. His 493 home runs put him in the Top 25 of all time, and his 1,995 runs batted in are surpassed only by Hank Aaron's 2,297 and Babe Ruth's 2,213. Then there was Gehrig's streak of 2,130 consecutive games played, a record that earned him another nickname: "The Iron Horse."

When ALS robbed Gehrig of his physical abilities, he said good-bye to baseball on July 4, 1939, with a Yankee Stadium address that featured the classic line, "Today I consider myself the luckiest man on the face of the earth." Honoring his fellow players as "grand men," his parents as "a blessing," and his wife as "a tower of strength," Gehrig departed with grace.

Grace—specifically God's grace—was the answer to the apostle Paul's incurable ailment. The great missionary pleaded with God three times to take away "a thorn in my flesh" (2 Corinthians 12:7–8), but he received an answer of no. What Paul did get was even better than a cure: God's promise, "My grace is sufficient for you, for my power is made perfect in weakness" (2 Corinthians 12:9).

Misfortune can knock down the strongest of men. But nothing can overpower God's grace.

*You then, my son, be strong in the grace that is in Christ Jesus.*
2 TIMOTHY 2:1

One more round tripper, and Andrés Galarraga would have joined the 400 home run club.

Not that 399 career homers are anything to be ashamed of—they rank

**JUST SHORT**

him in the Top 40 sluggers of all time, ahead of such notables as Joe DiMaggio, Johnny Bench, Jim Rice, Dave Parker, and Hank Greenberg. But many reports of the Big Cat's March 2005 retirement focused on the milestone missed, and the nineteen-year veteran himself had hoped to slam one more before hanging up his spikes. After a less-than-stellar spring training with the Mets, though, Galarraga decided his playing days were over and announced his retirement.

Over nearly two decades in the major leagues, Galarraga played for Montreal, St. Louis, Colorado, Atlanta, Texas, San Francisco, and Anaheim. He earned five All-Star selections, leading the league in hits and doubles (184 and 42, respectively) in 1988, batting average (.370) in 1993, runs batted in (150 and 140) in 1996 and '97, and home runs (47) in 1996. But one dream—hitting 400 career home runs—was not to be.

It's fine to have goals and make plans. Jesus Himself once mentioned a person considering a construction project: "Won't you first sit down and estimate the cost to see if you have enough money to complete it?" (Luke 14:28). But as we dream our dreams and pursue our desires, we should realize that, ultimately, it's God who gives or withholds success. As Solomon says in Proverbs 19:21, "Many are the plans in a person's heart, but it is the LORD's purpose that prevails."

Wild success, miserable failure, or falling just short—in the end, God makes the call.

> *Instead, you ought to say, "If it is the Lord's will, we will live and do this or that."*
> JAMES 4:15

# MARK TEIXEIRA

**Born:** April 11, 1980
**Height:** 6' 3"
**Weight:** 220 pounds
**Throws:** Right
**Bats:** Both

**Quote:** "Baseball is a game of failure. There are plenty of opportunities to be down, to feel sorry for yourself . . . but when you have God in your life and follow Christ, you're never going to be let down. Every time you fail, He's there to pick you right back up."

## MAJOR LEAGUE RECORD

*Drafted:* 1st round (5th overall) by Texas Rangers, 2001

*MLB debut:* April 1, 2003 (age 22), with Texas Rangers

*Stat highlights:* 43 home runs, 144 RBIs, 194 hits (2005), 45 doubles (2006), .308 batting average (2008)

Pit Willie Mays against Mickey Mantle in the World Series, and what do you get? Perhaps not the fireworks you'd expect.

Twice in their storied careers did the Say Hey Kid and the Commerce Comet match up in the Fall Classic—as rookies in 1951 and as seasoned veterans in 1962. Twice these huge stars disappointed.

**NOT TO THE STRONG**

In their combined careers, Mays and Mantle totaled forty years of Major League Baseball, thirty-six All-Star selections, eight home run titles, and four RBI crowns. Together they belted 1,196 home runs (660 for Mays and 536 for Mantle) and finished with lifetime batting averages right near .300—Mays at .302, Mantle at .298. Both were elected to the Hall of Fame in their first year of eligibility.

So what happened in the '51 and '62 World Series? When playing against each other's teams in the biggest games of all—thirteen total—they had a combined *two* RBIs without a single home run.

"The race is not to the swift or the battle to the strong," a wise man once wrote (Ecclesiastes 9:11). What we might expect or desire isn't always what God has planned. Consider King David being told he couldn't build God's temple (see 1 Chronicles 22) or the apostle Paul being prevented from preaching in Bithynia (see Acts 16). In fact, some of God's ways may seem a little strange—even very strange.

But God doesn't need "strong men" for His purposes—He can use any willing person to accomplish His plans. How about you?

> *My flesh and my heart may fail, but God is the strength of my heart and my portion forever.*
> PSALM 73:26

Before becoming a famous preacher, Billy Sunday was one of the fastest men in baseball.

He wasn't the greatest player of his generation. The outfielder nicknamed "The Evangelist" never played a full season and finished his eight-year major league career with a .248 batting average. Sunday hit only 12 career home runs during the "dead ball" era, and his fielding average was an anemic .883.

**RUNNER**

But the Iowa native could run. Sunday, who came up with the Chicago White Stockings, swiped a base in almost every other game he played—246 steals in 499 career games. In 1890, his final season, he stole 84 bases in 117 games with the National League's Pittsburgh and Philadelphia clubs, a performance ranking him near the Top 50 of all time.

Running is a key element of baseball but probably not something most people expect from God. If you read Jesus' parable of the lost (or "prodigal") son, though, you'll find an amazing picture of God the Father rushing to meet a repentant child.

A selfish young man, so the story goes, left home and wasted his generous father's wealth in wild living. After spending himself into a lonely bankruptcy, the son realized he belonged at home and decided to beg his father's forgiveness.

But, Jesus said, before the prodigal even reached home, "while he was still a long way off, his father saw him and was filled with compassion for him; he ran to his son, threw his arms around him and kissed him" (Luke 15:20).

Imagine the love of a father who *runs* to forgive the son who failed him. Through Jesus, you can enjoy that love today.

*As a father has compassion on his children, so the LORD has compassion on those who fear him; for he knows how we are formed, he remembers that we are dust.*
PSALM 103:13–14

Baseball today is much the same game Babe Ruth played. But, inevitably, time brings certain changes—to the chagrin of baseball purists.

By definition, a *purist* is a person who holds on strictly, even excessively, to tradition. Baseball purists believe innovation detracts from the "purity" of the game.

**PURISTS**

What kind of innovation? Things like night games, initiated by the Cincinnati Reds in 1935. Things like expansion, such as the addition of the New York Mets, Houston Colt 45s, Los Angeles Angels, Washington Senators, Kansas City Royals, Seattle Pilots, Montreal Expos, and San Diego Padres throughout the 1960s. Things like indoor baseball and artificial turf, innovations of the renamed Houston franchise that opened the Astrodome in 1965.

Then there was divisional play that began in 1969, and the move to three divisions in each league—with a playoff wild card team—beginning in 1994. The designated hitter appeared in the American League in 1973, while nearly a quarter century later—in 1997—American League and National League teams began meeting during the regular season in "interleague" play.

Those concerns of the baseball purists are open to debate. But there's no question that we as Christians should be "purists"—in the sense of moral and spiritual uprightness. Writing to the troubled church at Corinth, the apostle Paul said, "Since we have these promises, dear friends, let us purify ourselves from everything that contaminates body and spirit, perfecting holiness out of reverence for God" (2 Corinthians 7:1).

When Paul said "everything," he meant *everything*—whatever temptations, pursuits, and philosophies would draw us away from the Lord. Purity is fundamental.

*We know that when Christ appears, we shall be like him, for we shall see him as he is. All who have this hope in him purify themselves, just as he is pure.*

1 JOHN 3:2–3

Most players who retire with 14 career home runs and a lifetime batting average of .200 will be little remembered in five years, let alone forty. But most players aren't Bob Uecker.

As a catcher, Uecker performed well behind the plate, but *at* the plate, as a batter, it was another story entirely. He played in six major league seasons for St. Louis, Philadelphia, and both the Milwaukee and Atlanta Braves, dribbling out hits in limited plate appearances. In his busiest year, with the Phillies in 1966, Uecker hit .208 in 207 at bats. Twice he ended his season in buck-and-change territory.

**THE JOKER**

Always a joker, Uecker turned his meager baseball accomplishments into a shtick that brought him wide fame years after his playing career ended. Who can forget that line from a beer commercial, "I must be in the front rooow!"? Uecker had found his true stardom as a baseball comedian.

By definition, the "stars" of the world—in sports, business, politics, even Christianity—will be few and far between. But that's no reason for us .200 hitters to pack up our bats and go home. Take a cue from the joker and enjoy life whatever your status—superstar or average joe. It was the wisest man in human history, Solomon, who said, "A cheerful heart is good medicine" (Proverbs 17:22). That sounds a whole lot better than the second half of the verse: "but a crushed spirit dries up the bones."

Bob Uecker had it right: attitude makes a huge difference in our ultimate success.

*Rejoice in the LORD and be glad, you righteous;*
*sing, all you who are upright in heart!*
PSALM 32:11

Every team needs a utility man, the guy who can sub at most any position. During a twelve-year career, Cesar Tovar fit the bill for the Twins, Phillies, Rangers, A's, and Yankees.

## WHEREVER NEEDED

Born in Caracas, Venezuela, Tovar broke into the bigs with Minnesota in 1965. His inaugural season was a portent of things to come: he appeared four times at second base, twice at third, twice in center field, and once at shortstop.

The next season, "Pepito's" game total jumped to 134 with 76 games at second base, 31 at shortstop, four in left field, and 20 in center. By his third year, Tovar played a league-high 164 games for the Twins at second, third, short, and all three outfield positions.

With the '68 Twins, Tovar actually played every position on the field. That feat is even more notable when you realize he played them all in a single game. Not surprisingly, it happened late in the season on September 22 against Oakland. While pitching, he struck out the great Reggie Jackson.

Though for the next four years Tovar played primarily outfield (including the 1971 season when he led the American League with 204 hits), the final third of his career featured a variety of positions once again, including a new role: designated hitter. Being willing and able to play wherever needed was a big factor in Cesar Tovar's success.

God is looking for that "wherever needed" kind of person, too—the kind the apostle Paul described in his second letter to the Corinthian Christians: "And God is able to bless you abundantly, so that in all things at all times, having all that you need, you will abound in every good work" (2 Corinthians 9:8).

Whenever, wherever, however, God has a job for you. Are you ready to serve?

*I thank Christ Jesus our Lord, who has given me strength,*
*that he considered me trustworthy, appointing me to his service.*
1 TIMOTHY 1:12

Every organization needs someone with authority. For a baseball team, that's the manager—or at least it should be.

While tensions between managers and players are not uncommon, the 1940 Cleveland Indians took their frustration with manager Ossie Vitt to an extreme. They tried to get him fired.

**AUTHORITY**

The season started well for the Tribe, with Opening Day pitcher Bob Feller no-hitting the White Sox 1–0. Cleveland and Detroit, taking advantage of a poor start by the New York Yankees, jockeyed for the league lead throughout the season. But late in the year, the Indians lost five straight games, including three to the rival Tigers, and ended up one game back of the Bengals in the final standings. Cleveland missed a chance at a first-ever all-Ohio World Series as the Cincinnati Reds won the National League crown.

The Indians' slide may have resulted from a clubhouse distraction—a rebellion against their third-year skipper. Though Vitt led Cleveland to a winning record each season—with 86, 87, and 89 victories, respectively—the players resented his authoritarian rule. When they unsuccessfully petitioned club ownership to can Vitt, they earned the nickname "The Cry Babies."

Biblical writers would have looked askance at the Indians' complaints. "Have confidence in your leaders and submit to their authority," said the writer of Hebrews, "because they keep watch over you as those who must give an account. Do this so that their work will be a joy, not a burden, for that would be of no benefit to you" (Hebrews 13:17).

Good, bad, or indifferent, the authorities in our lives should be obeyed.

*Slaves, obey your earthly masters in everything; and do it,*
*not only when their eye is on you and to curry their favor,*
*but with sincerity of heart and reverence for the Lord.*
COLOSSIANS 3:22

What if you could assemble a team from the greatest players of all time?

On the field, of course, it would be impossible. But it's an interesting exercise on paper—one that Major League Baseball organized in 1999 as "The All-Century Team."

## THE DREAM TEAM

Check out this star-studded lineup: pitchers Nolan Ryan, Sandy Koufax, Cy Young, Roger Clemens, Bob Gibson, Walter Johnson, Warren Spahn, Christy Mathewson, and Lefty Grove; catchers Johnny Bench and Yogi Berra; first basemen Lou Gehrig and Mark McGwire (obviously before the revelations of his performance-enhancing drug use); second basemen Jackie Robinson and Rogers Hornsby; third basemen Mike Schmidt and Brooks Robinson; shortstops Cal Ripken Jr., Ernie Banks, and Honus Wagner; and outfielders Babe Ruth, Hank Aaron, Ted Williams, Willie Mays, Joe DiMaggio, Mickey Mantle, Ty Cobb, Ken Griffey Jr., Pete Rose, and Stan Musial.

That's an imposing lineup, featuring the all-time leaders in wins (Young), strikeouts thrown (Ryan), RBIs (Aaron), hits (Rose), batting average (Cobb), and consecutive games played (Ripken). Wearing the same uniform, those thirty players would form a nearly invincible team.

Christians form a pretty tough team, too, backed by our all-powerful God. Working together, we can accomplish amazing things—like the ancient Israelites' victory over the Amalekites at a place called Rephidim. There Moses held the "staff of God" over the battlefield, causing success until his arms sagged. Then, "when Moses' hands grew tired, they took a stone and put it under him and he sat on it. Aaron and Hur held his hands up—one on one side, one on the other—so that his hands remained steady till sunset. So Joshua overcame the Amalekite army with the sword" (Exodus 17:12–13).

You, your fellow Christians, and God—that's the ultimate "Dream Team."

*I planted the seed, Apollos watered it,*
*but God has been making it grow.*
1 CORINTHIANS 3:6

For many fans, poring over the statistics of baseball is just as enjoyable as watching a game.

The numbers and their various combinations seem endless. First, there's the raw data: for teams, total wins and losses; for players, everything from at bats, home runs, strikeouts, and stolen bases to innings pitched, shutouts, saves, and balks. Then there are the averages, based on multiple factors like base hits and official at bats (for batting average), times on base and total plate appearances (for on-base percentage), or earned runs and innings pitched (for earned run average).

**STATISTICS**

Broadcasters often crunch numbers to create impressive credentials for the player they're describing at the moment: "Clutch Smith is leading the league this year while batting left-handed with two outs in the ninth inning and his team trailing by a run."

Baseball's statistics are kept for individual players, for teams, and even for the game as a whole. In 1975, for example, Major League Baseball noted that Bob Watson, a first baseman and outfielder with the Houston Astros, had scored the one millionth run in big league history. Someone was keeping track.

According to the Bible, God seems to enjoy statistics, too. "He determines the number of the stars," the psalmist wrote, "and calls them each by name" (Psalm 147:4). Jesus once told His disciples, "Even the very hairs of your head are all numbered" (Matthew 10:30).

Why would God keep such figures? For one thing, they prove His complete knowledge of everything in the entire universe—which should give you hope in your own little corner of the world.

*"Are not two sparrows sold for a penny? Yet not one of them will fall to the ground outside your Father's care. . . . So don't be afraid; you are worth more than many sparrows."*
MATTHEW 10:29, 31

For more than a century, the World Series has been the pinnacle of professional baseball achievement. So why would a Major League official publicly downplay the event?

## OUR MODEST LITTLE SPORTING EVENT

Here are some hints: the comment was made during the 1989 championship. The teams involved were the Oakland A's and San Francisco Giants.

If you were a fan at that time, you probably recall this "Bay Area World Series" for the interruption of a 7.1 magnitude earthquake. More than sixty Californians died and billions of dollars in damage resulted.

The temblor struck just before Game 3 in San Francisco, with the A's up two games to none. Though there were no injuries at Candlestick Park, baseball officials delayed the series out of respect for victims throughout the Bay Area. Ten days would pass before the series resumed with Oakland proceeding to sweep the Giants in what commissioner Fay Vincent called "our modest little sporting event."

When tragedies strike, people often ask, "Why?" We like to have reasons for the hardships that befall ourselves and others. One temptation is to presume that those trials are the result of sin. But Jesus Himself, referring to a "news item" of His day, argued against that assumption: "Those eighteen who died when the tower in Siloam fell on them—do you think they were more guilty than all the others living in Jerusalem? I tell you, no!" (Luke 13:4–5).

Tragedy and hardship, in Jesus' view, should point us to the larger realities of life. The point of His story in Luke 13 was this: "But unless you repent, you too will all perish." In John 9 Jesus said human hardship can show the power of God.

That's more important than any modest little sporting event.

*"Neither this man nor his parents sinned," said Jesus, "but this happened so that the works of God might be displayed in him."*

JOHN 9:3

Competing teams, it is said, "share the field." That phrase took on a whole new meaning in St. Louis in 1944.

For more than three decades, from 1920 to 1953, the National League Cardinals and American League Browns both called Sportsman's Park home. Also known at times as Busch Stadium and Steininger Field, the ballpark held more than thirty thousand Gateway City fans.

## SHARING THE FIELD

Of the two teams, the Cardinals enjoyed much greater success there. The National Leaguers were often a first-division team and had several World Series appearances to their credit. From 1942–44, with Stan Musial leading the way, the Cards won three straight National League pennants, racking up at least 105 wins each season.

The Browns were perennial doormats but turned World War II to their advantage by winning the 1944 American League crown. When military call-ups decimated other teams' rosters, the Browns cobbled together a squad that won St. Louis' sole American League championship. The first and only all–St. Louis World Series was played—like all of the Browns' and Cardinals' games that season—in Sportsman's Park, where the Cardinals took the championship in six games.

A quirk of baseball fate allowed two St. Louis teams to share the field for the 1944 postseason—but careful planning accounted for their sharing the same stadium for more than thirty years. Conscious sharing should be a hallmark of our Christian lives, too, as the writer of Hebrews once noted: "Do not forget to do good and to share with others, for with such sacrifices God is pleased" (Hebrews 13:16).

Money, talent, energy, time—whatever is needed, be willing to give.

*Share with the Lord's people who are in need.*
*Practice hospitality.*
ROMANS 12:13

# MATT CAPPS

**Born:** September 3, 1983
**Height:** 6' 2"
**Weight:** 245 pounds
**Throws:** Right
**Bats:** Right

**Quote:** "I know that God loves me and there's a purpose for me being here. There's a reason why I struggle. There's a reason why I have success. And it's not really for me or you to understand. There's a greater reason, a better reason, for me to be on this earth. Baseball is the resource God has put in front of me to spread the Gospel and make other people aware."

## MAJOR LEAGUE RECORD

*Drafted:* 7th round by Pittsburgh Pirates, 2002

*MLB debut:* September 16, 2005 (age 22), with Pittsburgh Pirates

*Stat highlights:* 9–1 record (2006), 42 saves, 2.47 ERA (2010)

Rules, some argue, are made to be broken. That's a philosophy followed by certain major league pitchers.

Baseball's rule book contains some very detailed instruction on what a pitcher may *not* do with a baseball: expectorate on it, rub it on his glove or clothing, apply any foreign substance to it, or deface it in any other way. If a pitcher delivers a spit-, shine, mud, or emery ball, the rules say he should immediately be ejected and suspended for ten games.

**SNEAKY PITCHES**

But neither the rules nor the prescribed punishment stop some pitchers from doctoring the ball in search of an advantage over the hitter. According to the website baseball-reference.com, the game's "Famous and Accused Doctorers of Baseballs" in recent years include Joe Niekro, Gaylord Perry, Rick Honeycutt, Don Sutton, and David Wells. If actually guilty, the famous and accused have found great success: Perry and Sutton are members of the Hall of Fame, and Wells owns the modern era's thirteenth perfect game.

Sneaky pitches might advance a baseball career, but cheating is completely off-limits to the Christian. God's standard is doing the right thing every time, as the apostle Paul wrote to a coworker named Titus: "In everything set them an example by doing what is good. In your teaching show integrity, seriousness and soundness of speech that cannot be condemned, so that those who oppose you may be ashamed because they have nothing bad to say about us" (Titus 2:7–8).

Never be a "famous or accused" practitioner of anything questionable. Don't let a sneaky pitch hurt your reputation as a follower of Jesus.

*Reject every kind of evil.*
1 THESSALONIANS 5:22

As one of baseball's biggest stars, Christy Mathewson was pushing forty when he left to serve in the "Great War," which we know as World War I.

Nicknamed "Big Six" (short for "Big Six-Footer," which shows how much athletes' physiques have changed in a hundred years), Mathewson enjoyed a seventeen-year major league career, winning 373 games, third most all-time. His 79 shutouts rank second all-time, and his career earned run average of 2.13 is good for fifth. None of Mathewson's totals appear likely to be surpassed.

**FOR THE CAUSE**

The New York Giant right-hander notched four seasons with at least 30 victories, winning a remarkable 37 in 1908. That season, when he posted a 1.43 ERA, is noted on his plaque at the Baseball Hall of Fame in Cooperstown, New York. Christy Mathewson was part of the very first group of honorees in 1939.

Sadly, he was unable to attend the induction ceremony, having died fourteen years earlier from complications of tuberculosis. Exposure to poison gas during his military service may have been the reason for the illness. Big Six had given his all for the cause.

In the cause of Christ, Jesus promised that all sacrifices would be generously rewarded. "Truly I tell you," He said, "no one who has left home or brothers or sisters or mother or father or children or fields for me and the gospel will fail to receive a hundred times as much in this present age . . . and in the age to come, eternal life" (Mark 10:29–30).

In God's worldwide family, there are countless fellow believers who can provide whatever spiritual, emotional, physical, and even financial support we need. When you give to Jesus' cause, you open the door to God's blessing.

> *"Look, I am coming soon! My reward is with me, and I will give to each person according to what they have done."*
> REVELATION 22:12

When an average guy does something extraordinary, befuddled observers may have questions—not all of them bright.

Don Larsen was an average guy. As a rookie pitcher with the St. Louis Browns in 1953, the 6-foot, 4-inch right-hander went 7–12 with a 4.16 earned run average. The next year, when the Brownies moved to Baltimore to become the Orioles, Larsen went along, too—suffering through an abysmal 3–21 season.

**DUMB QUESTION**

Still, you have to be viewed as a decent pitcher to stick around after losing more than twenty games—and Larsen's fortunes began to turn as a member of the Yankees in 1955. He trimmed more than a run off his ERA, finishing 9–2 for the pennant-winning pinstripes. Another good season followed as Larsen's 11–5 record helped the Yanks to yet another American League championship. That 1956 win total would be the high point in a fourteen-year big league career.

Facing Brooklyn in the World Series, Larsen got knocked around in Game 2, losing 13–8. But in Game 5, with the series tied at two games each, Don Larsen won baseball immortality by tossing a perfect game. His performance was so shocking that a certain sportswriter might be forgiven his dumb postgame question: "Is that the best game you ever pitched?"

Another "dumb question" once came from the mouth of a Jewish ruler who visited Jesus. When Christ said, "No one can see the kingdom of God unless they are born again" (John 3:3), Nicodemus responded, "How can someone be born when they are old? . . . Surely they cannot enter a second time into their mother's womb to be born!" (John 3:4). Without the required spiritual understanding, Nicodemus was baffled by Jesus' words.

If God's Word confuses you, maybe you need the Author's insights. Ask God for His Spirit to explain it.

*The person without the Spirit does not accept the things that come from the Spirit of God but considers them foolishness, and cannot understand them because they are discerned only through the Spirit.*
1 CORINTHIANS 2:14

Sprinkled throughout the pages of baseball history are the occasional "one day wonders"—guys who got a single shot in the big leagues and made the most of it.

## BRIEF BUT PRODUCTIVE

Consider Mike Hopkins, a catcher who played one day, August 24, 1902, with the Pittsburgh Pirates. The native of Glasgow, Scotland, had two at bats, recording a single and a double—then never played again. He "retired" with a career batting average and on-base percentage of 1.000 and a slugging average of 1.500.

Roe Skidmore reached the Big Show on September 17, 1970, with the Chicago Cubs. In his one at bat, he slapped a single—and promptly exited the game with a batting average, on-base percentage, and slugging average of 1.000.

Hank Schmulbach's only appearance in the major leagues came with the St. Louis Browns on September 27, 1943. Brought in as a pinch runner, he came around to score—then never played again in a big league contest.

As baseball careers go, each was brief but productive. They suggest a parallel to the ministry of God's Son.

Over the course of about three years, Jesus trained disciples, performed miracles, taught crowds, and set an example for every generation to follow. What made his brief "career" so productive? An unflinching focus on doing God's will: " 'My food,' said Jesus, 'is to do the will of him who sent me and to finish his work' " (John 4:34).

God gives most of us much more than a single day or even three years. Will you make your spiritual "career" productive by doing His will?

*"I desire to do your will, my God;*
*your law is within my heart."*
PSALM 40:8

Is there such a thing as a "crystal (base) ball"?

Since the game's earliest years, managers, scouts, and executives have tried to guess players' futures—whether a young prospect had major league potential, whether a breakout season represented true talent or just luck, whether it was worth signing an aging veteran.

**PROJECTIONS**

Often, those calls are simply gut feelings. But a breed of number crunchers has developed entire systems of projection, to try to predict the future for major leaguers. *Baseball Prospectus,* for example, offered up the following predictions for Clayton Kershaw, who won the 2011 National League Cy Young Award with a 21–5 record and 2.28 ERA: for 2012, Kershaw was projected to go 12–9 with a 2.71 ERA, striking out 180 over 190 ⅓ innings. What was the 2012 reality? Kershaw went 14–9 with a 2.53 ERA, striking out 229 over 227 ⅔ innings. The projection was in the ballpark, maybe, but hardly the advertised "deadly accurate" for a pitcher who would go on to capture his second Cy Young Award in 2013 following his stellar 16–9 record and 1.83 ERA.

How about Cincinnati's All-Star first baseman Joey Votto? *Baseball Prospectus* slated him for 661 plate appearances, 33 home runs, and 103 RBIs in 2012. The actual stats: 475 plate appearances, 14 home runs, and 56 RBIs. What the prognosticators missed was that Votto would lose 51 games due to injury.

Baseball projections—like most predictions in life—are simply guesswork. But the Bible's projection in Galatians 6:7 is true every time: "Do not be deceived: God cannot be mocked. A man reaps what he sows."

It's good to view that from the negative side: Seeds of dishonesty, anger, or adultery lead to a terrible harvest, and we should avoid all of them. But there's a positive side, too: Seeds of honesty, kindness, and purity result in a healthy crop that benefits our lives.

No guesswork involved.

*Whoever sows to please their flesh, from the flesh will reap destruction; whoever sows to please the Spirit, from the Spirit will reap eternal life.*
GALATIANS 6:8

Like a stick of dynamite, Albie Pearson held a lot of energy in a small package.

Born Albert Gregory Pearson in Alhambra, California, "Albie" topped out at 5 feet, 5 inches in height when he stopped growing. But his short stature had no ill effect on his baseball ability.

**THE LITTLE GUY**

He entered the big leagues in 1958 as an outfielder with the Washington Senators. Pearson's rookie season featured a .275 batting average on 146 hits in 530 at bats. Twenty-five doubles, five triples, and three home runs, combined with his 63 runs scored, helped the first-year American Leaguer to win the Rookie of the Year award. He was the smallest man ever so honored.

Though Pearson struggled over the next two seasons—his batting average dipped to .216 in 1959—he found his groove again with the expansion Los Angeles Angels in '61 when he batted .288. The following season, he led the league in runs scored with 115, and the year after that batted .304 and earned an All-Star appearance. Not bad for a little guy.

Neither did stature matter when the prophet Samuel sought a replacement for Israel's first king, Saul. At God's direction, Samuel reviewed the eight sons of a man named Jesse—and adjusted his expectations based on the Lord's response to the first: "Do not consider his appearance or his height, for I have rejected him. The LORD does not look at the things people look at. People look at the outward appearance, but the LORD looks at the heart" (1 Samuel 16:7).

The old saying is true: It's what's inside that counts. If you ever need a reminder, think of Albie Pearson.

(Bonus information: Albie went into ministry after his baseball career and founded a home for abused, neglected, and abandoned young boys.)

*Jesus said to them, ". . . Stop judging by mere appearances, but instead judge correctly."*
JOHN 7:21, 24

Great nicknames fill the pages of baseball history books.

Most every fan knows the old-time nicknames like George Herman "Babe" Ruth, "Shoeless Joe" Jackson, "Joltin' Joe" DiMaggio, and "Stan the Man" Musial. In the 1970s, there was Jim "Catfish" Hunter, "Mr. October" Reggie Jackson, Willie "Pops" Stargell, and "The Eck," Dennis Eckersley. More recently, in the early '00s, "Big" was big, with Frank "The Big Hurt" Thomas, Mark "Big Mac" McGwire, and Randy "The Big Unit" Johnson.

**NICKNAMES**

Some of baseball's more memorable nicknames have hung on relatively forgettable players. Take, for example, Ed "The Midget" Mensor, who compiled a .221 lifetime batting average for Pittsburgh from 1912 to 1914. Or Benny "Earache" Meyer, who played for three teams in a three-year career—or four teams in a four-year career, if you count a single at bat for the Phillies in 1925, a decade after his last regular game. Then there's George Miller, who hit .267 over thirteen years in the late 1800s. He may win the prize for most nicknames, going by "Doggie," "Foghorn," and "Calliope" at various times.

Clearly, nicknames are nothing new. Jesus Himself once assigned one to a couple of His disciples, the brothers James and John: "to them he gave the name Boanerges, which means 'sons of thunder' " (Mark 3:17).

What was that all about? Maybe it referred to the hot temper they showed in suggesting the destruction of a Samaritan town that had disrespected Jesus (Luke 9:51–55). In time, though, James gave his life out of dedication to Christ and John became the "apostle of love."

Are you a son of thunder? Or a son of anger, pride, fear, or resentment? Take encouragement from James and John. That nickname isn't the final word.

*Do not conform to the pattern of this world,*
*but be transformed by the renewing of your mind.*
Romans 12:2

It's fitting that a man nicknamed "The Lip" would produce one of the most enduring quotations of baseball.

As manager of the Brooklyn Dodgers in 1946, Leo Durocher was asked

**NICE GUYS**

his opinion of the crosstown New York Giants. "They're nice guys," Durocher said. "They'll probably finish last." Newspapers picked up the comment, shortening the seven words to a succinct and memorable four: "Nice guys finish last."

Durocher, formerly a shortstop with the Murderer's Row Yankees and the Gashouse Gang Cardinals, apparently knew what he was saying: the Giants did finish last in 1946. Two years later, those same Giants brought The Lip on as manager, and by 1954 (presumably now as mean and angry guys), they were World Series champions.

Whether nicety is truly the cause of last-place finishes is a matter of debate. But the reality of each baseball season, and of most every endeavor of life, is that somebody will finish last. Nobody wants to be a loser—but even that concept of *losing* is open to debate.

In the Christian life, so full of paradoxes, losers are winners. What is lost is found. Weakness is strength. Remember these verses? "I consider everything a loss because of the surpassing worth of knowing Christ Jesus my Lord" (Philippians 3:8). "Whoever loses their life for my sake will find it" (Matthew 10:39). "For Christ's sake, I delight in weaknesses, in insults, in hardships, in persecutions, in difficulties. For when I am weak, then I am strong" (2 Corinthians 12:10).

The point is this: be a "nice guy"—the faithful Christian. There's more to that last-place finish than meets the eye.

> *Jesus called the Twelve and said, "Anyone who wants to be first must be the very last, and the servant of all."*
> MARK 9:35

Lacking a play clock, baseball games can unfold at a leisurely pace. Pitchers and hitters often take their time, few perhaps more than Mike Hargrove did.

Years before his successful managing stint with the Cleveland Indians, Hargrove played first base and outfield for the Tribe, Padres, and Rangers. In twelve big league seasons, the man from Perryton, Texas, recorded nearly a thousand bases on balls, including league-leading totals with the Rangers in 1976 and '78 (97 and 107, respectively). Four times Hargrove had more than 100 walks in a season, reaching a high of 111 with Cleveland in 1980.

**THE CLOCK**

His methodical approach to batting yielded a career on-base percentage of .396, among the Top 100 in history, and earned Hargrove a nickname for all that time he spent in the batter's box: The Human Rain Delay.

Delaying may be a good tactic for hitters, but it's not productive in the Christian life. The apostle Paul, urging wholehearted service to God, warned the church in Corinth that "the time is short. From now on those who have wives should live as if they do not; those who mourn, as if they did not; those who are happy, as if they were not; those who buy something, as if it were not theirs to keep; those who use the things of the world, as if not engrossed in them. For this world in its present form is passing away" (1 Corinthians 7:29–31).

Paul's point? Nothing—not even your most important human relationships—compares with your duty to God, and you don't have the luxury of time. Unlike the game of baseball, life has a clock.

*You have made my days a mere handbreadth; the span of*
*my years is as nothing before you. Everyone is but a breath.*
PSALM 39:5

Hank Aaron's home run record lasted thirty-three years. Then Barry Bonds came along.

"Hammerin' Hank," of course, had taken the record from the legendary Babe Ruth, whose mark of 714 stood for thirty-nine years—from 1935 until 1974. After breaking the Bambino's record, Aaron added 40 more dingers, retiring with 755 in 1976.

**HOME RUN KINGS**

Ten years after that, Bonds broke into the big leagues with the Pittsburgh Pirates. He swatted 16 home runs his rookie year then 25 in his sophomore campaign. In 1993, his first year with the San Francisco Giants, Bonds tied for the major league lead with 46 homers. Seasons of 37, 33, 42, 40, 37, 34, and 49 home runs followed before the big left fielder set the all-time single season mark of 73 in 2001. (In recent years, of course, that record has been discredited as a by-product of baseball's "steroid era" and widely criticized by fans and baseball historians alike.)

Bonds continued his assault on Aaron's record and finally surpassed him on August 7, 2007. Facing the Washington Nationals' Mike Bacsik, Bonds launched number 756 to become baseball's all-time home run king—maybe.

Under normal circumstances, it's nice to be a "king"—an acknowledged leader in sports, business, politics, or other field of human endeavor. But no matter how high we rise, there's always Someone higher: Jesus Christ. "He is dressed in a robe dipped in blood, and his name is the Word of God. . . . On his robe and on his thigh he has this name written: KING OF KINGS AND LORD OF LORDS" (Revelation 19:13, 16).

Always keep your eyes on the real King—and doing what's right.

*"You are a king, then!" said Pilate. Jesus answered, "You say that I am a king. In fact, the reason I was born and came into the world is to testify to the truth. Everyone on the side of truth listens to me."*
JOHN 18:37

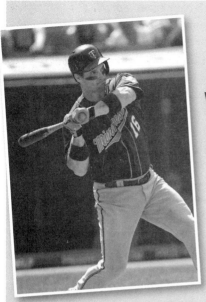

# JOSH WILLINGHAM

**Born:** February 17, 1979
**Height:** 6' 2"
**Weight:** 215 pounds
**Throws:** Right
**Bats:** Right

**Quote:** "I don't understand how people do it if they don't have faith, especially [regarding] eternal life. What kind of hope do people have? You have to really lean on God when a trial happens. He has basically showed me that he is the boss through difficult times."

## MAJOR LEAGUE RECORD

*Drafted:* 17th round by Florida Marlins, 2000

*MLB debut:* July 6, 2004 (age 25), with Florida Marlins

*Stat highlights:* 32 doubles (2007), 35 home runs (2010), 110 RBIs (2012)

He was good enough to reach the major leagues, but not good enough to stay long. Yet he'll always be good enough in the record books.

Confused? It's a baseball riddle, of sorts.

**GOOD ENOUGH?**

The answer is Bill Goodenough, who appeared in 10 games for the 1893 St. Louis Cardinals. The 6-foot, 1-inch, 170-pound center fielder was a late-season call-up for the Cards, debuting on August 31 for a squad that would finish tenth in the twelve-team National League.

Goodenough's statistics were as mundane as his team's performance that year. In 31 at bats, he rapped only four singles and a double for a batting average of .161. He reached base six other times—equally divided between walks and hit by pitches—stole a pair of bases, and scored four runs. And then Bill Goodenough, apparently not good enough, disappeared from the major leagues.

We might play off Mr. Goodenough's story to encourage people to try a little harder, live a little better, strive a little more to be "good enough" to please God. But that really misses the point.

The apostle Paul wrote to Christians in Rome that "no one will be declared righteous in God's sight by the works of the law" (Romans 3:20). Our good works aren't what please God—it's what we believe about the life, death, and resurrection of Jesus. As Paul asked the Galatians, "Did you receive the Spirit by the works of the law, or by believing what you heard?" (Galatians 3:2).

It's good to do good, but never think that's your ticket to heaven. Only faith in Jesus makes you "good enough."

*Where, then, is boasting? It is excluded. Because of what law? The law that requires works? No, because of the law that requires faith. For we maintain that a person is justified by faith apart from the works of the law.*
ROMANS 3:27–28

Tommy Glaviano made his mark on baseball in a way he probably wishes he hadn't.

In a five-year major league career, the native of Sacramento, California, played primarily infield positions for the St. Louis Cardinals and Philadelphia Phillies. His batting average was, well, average—a lifetime figure of .257. In 389 games, he had just over a thousand at bats, notching 259 hits and 24 career home runs.

**ERROR, ERROR, ERROR**

But Glaviano, whose nickname was "Rabbit," earned his most lasting fame at third base. While playing the hot corner for the Cards against the Brooklyn Dodgers on May 18, 1950, he committed errors on three straight plays.

Fielders hate to be charged with errors at all, and two in a game can be mortifying. But errors on three consecutive plays? In baseball, that's almost unforgivable.

For us as Christians, though, nothing is "unforgivable," according to Jesus. After telling His disciples how to handle fellow believers who might sin against them, Peter asked Jesus, "Lord, how many times shall I forgive my brother or sister who sins against me? Up to seven times?" (Matthew 18:21).

"Seven times" probably seemed generous to Peter—until Jesus replied, "I tell you, not seven times, but seventy-seven times" (Matthew 18:22). Some other versions of the Bible translate the number as "seventy times seven."

Whatever the number may be, it's a lot—and it's unlikely that Jesus was really telling us to keep count. The point is this: when other Christians commit errors against you, your responsibility is to forgive.

*Bear with each other and forgive one another if any of you has a grievance against someone. Forgive as the Lord forgave you.*
COLOSSIANS 3:13

For the United States' bicentennial year of 1976, the favored color scheme was red, white, and blue. In baseball that season, it was all red—as in Cincinnati Reds.

**THE MACHINE**

The Queen City boys, following their 1975 World Series triumph over Boston, won 102 games to take the National League West by 10 over Los Angeles. In the National League Championship Series, Cincinnati swept the Phillies—winners of 101 games themselves—earning a return trip to the Fall Classic. There the Reds dismantled the Yankees 5–1, 4–3, 6–2, and 7–2, as Johnny Bench collected eight hits—including a double, a triple, and a pair of home runs.

Cincinnati enjoyed great offense all season, leading the National League in almost every offensive category. They had 87 more runs, 94 more hits, 31 more home runs, and 60 more stolen bases than any other team on their way to a second straight championship. Things were clearly going the "Big Red Machine's" way.

Sometimes life goes our way—our health is good, our family is happy, our job is positive. But don't be surprised to discover the proverbial monkey wrench in your machine. "Everyone who wants to live a godly life in Christ Jesus will be persecuted," the apostle Paul wrote his friend and fellow pastor Timothy (2 Timothy 3:12). "In this world you will have trouble," Jesus once told His disciples (John 16:33).

What can put your "machine" back on track? Check out the rest of Jesus' comment in John 16:33: "But take heart! I have overcome the world."

*Dear friends, do not be surprised at the fiery ordeal that has come on you to test you, as though something strange were happening to you. But rejoice inasmuch as you participate in the sufferings of Christ, so that you may be overjoyed when his glory is revealed.*
1 PETER 4:12–13

Can a player make a name for himself toiling in the shadows of Ruth and Gehrig?

Tony Lazzeri did. As a member of the famed Yankee teams of the 1920s and '30s, Lazzeri played primarily at second base with occasional appearances at third and short.

**MORE THAN YOU'D IMAGINE**

Though the San Francisco native had once clubbed a Ruthian 60 home runs in a minor league season (with Salt Lake City in 1925), he never surpassed 18 in a major league campaign. He retired with a respectable, but not amazing, total of 178. And though he did have five seasons with a batting average over .300—including his personal best .354 in 1929—he finished with a respectable, but not amazing, career average of .292.

What *was* amazing was Lazzeri's performance on May 24, 1936, when he slugged two grand slams and knocked in an American League record 11 RBIs against the Philadelphia Athletics. That single-game statistic was so memorable it was cast in bronze on Lazzeri's plaque at the Baseball Hall of Fame in Cooperstown.

An 11-RBI performance was more than most would have imagined from Babe Ruth, let alone Lazzeri—just as Jesus' disciples couldn't imagine that five loaves and two fish would ever feed a crowd of 5,000 men. But they did.

After Jesus "gave thanks and broke the loaves . . . he also divided the two fish among them all" (Mark 6:41). Amazingly, "they all ate and were satisfied, and the disciples picked up twelve basketfuls of broken pieces of bread and fish" (Mark 6:42–43).

God enjoys doing more than we could ever imagine. What might you ask Him for today?

*Now to him who is able to do immeasurably more than all we ask or imagine . . . to him be glory in the church and in Christ Jesus throughout all generations, for ever and ever!*
Ephesians 3:20–21

Some of baseball's greatest careers began with a Rookie of the Year award. So did some flops.

Since 1947, the Baseball Writers Association of America has honored

**ROOKIE OF THE YEAR**

the first-year player who outpaces the rest of his class. The very first Rookie of the Year was the very first African-American in the modern major leagues, Jackie Robinson. The rest of the list, which in 1949 began honoring a player in each league, often reads like a Who's Who of current and probable Hall of Famers: Willie Mays, Tom Seaver, Rod Carew, Johnny Bench, Carlton Fisk, Fred Lynn, Mike Piazza, Derek Jeter—and the list goes on.

But a few Rookies of the Year make the average fan pause. Who was Don Schwall (American League, 1961) or Carl Morton (National League, 1970) or "Super Joe" Charbonneau (American League, 1980)?

Long-suffering Cleveland fans remember Charbonneau as a player of unfulfilled potential. The quirky outfielder appeared destined for stardom after batting .289 with 23 home runs his freshman season. By the middle of the following year, though, batting just over .200, "Super Joe" was back in the minors. Early in 1983, his professional career ended when he was released by Class AA Buffalo.

To be truly successful, we need to finish well—especially in the Christian life. The apostle Paul, who accomplished so much as a missionary and Bible writer, knew that to finish well he had to control the sinful physical desires that plagued him as much as they do us: "I strike a blow to my body and make it my slave so that after I have preached to others, I myself will not be disqualified for the prize" (1 Corinthians 9:27).

A good start is a wonderful thing. But a strong finish is what people really remember.

*Be alert and of sober mind. Your enemy the devil prowls around like a roaring lion looking for someone to devour.*

1 PETER 5:8

Base runners hate to make the last out of an inning—or worse, the final out of a game.

Old-fashioned blunders get some runners picked off, but for many, aggressiveness is the culprit—the desire to stretch a single into a double, a double into a triple, or a triple into an inside-the-park home run.

**STRETCHING FOR MORE**

An attempt to wring a double from a single ended the 2006 season opener between the Mets and Nationals. In the top of the ninth, New York led 3–2 when Washington second baseman Jose Vidro lashed a two-out hit to the left-center-field gap. The Mets' Carlos Beltran, though, quickly flagged down the ball and made a perfect throw to erase Vidro at second. Just like that—a possible rally . . . and the game . . . was over.

Isn't that the nature of temptation? We find ourselves reaching for things beyond the good that God has already given us. Eve could enjoy 99.99 percent of the Garden of Eden—but was caught stretching for a forbidden fruit. David had several wives—but stumbled stretching for Bathsheba. The Israelites were the chosen people of the one true God—but blew it, over and over again, stretching for idols. In every case, the results were disastrous.

That's why the Bible so often warns against temptation, that stretching for things we shouldn't have. "Do not offer any part of yourself to sin as an instrument of wickedness, but rather offer yourselves to God as those who have been brought from death to life; and offer every part of yourself to him as an instrument of righteousness" (Romans 6:13).

If you're going to be caught stretching for more, make sure it's for God.

*Do not set foot on the path of the wicked,*
*or walk in the way of evildoers.*
PROVERBS 4:14

Rainouts are a nuisance for most baseball fans. But for followers of the Boston Braves, they could be a godsend.

The Beantown crowd of the late 1940s even had a joking chant—"Spahn and Sain and pray for rain!"—that begged divine intervention on the days Boston's two star pitchers had off.

**PRAY FOR RAIN**

Warren Spahn and Johnny Sain began their careers with the Braves in 1942 then left the next season to serve in World War II. Safely back from the military in 1946, they led an otherwise mediocre Boston pitching staff to third- and fourth-place finishes—with the notable exception of the 1948 National League pennant—over the next half decade. Through 1951, the pair combined for eight 20-win seasons.

But with fellow starters like "Big Bill" Lee finishing 10–9 in 1946, Bill Voiselle going 28–28 from 1947 to 1949, and Bob Chipman posting a 14–15 record through the 1949 and 1950 seasons, Boston fans thought a timely shower from heaven might be just what the Braves' staff most needed.

We don't know if God really answered the Boston fans' prayers, but we can always be sure He'll take care of us. In the Sermon on the Mount, while teaching love for enemies, Jesus noted that God "causes his sun to rise on the evil and the good, and sends rain on the righteous and the unrighteous" (Matthew 5:45). Shortly afterward, He reminded His followers not to worry about food, drink, or clothing, because "your heavenly Father knows that you need them" (Matthew 6:32).

In sunshine or rain, Boston or anywhere else, God is always watching out for His children.

*Every good and perfect gift is from above,*
*coming down from the Father of the heavenly*
*lights, who does not change like shifting shadows.*
JAMES 1:17

The fireworks came a day early for Atlanta Braves' pitcher Tony Cloninger.

On July 3, 1966, the 6-foot right-hander did something rather unpitcherlike: he hit two grand slams in a game against San Francisco, which the Braves won 17–3. Cloninger's one-day take of nine RBIs (he singled home another run) would be considered a great *week* for most position players.

**SURPRISING STRENGTH**

For a pitcher at the plate, Cloninger had a pretty good year in '66. In his sixth year with the Braves, having just come south with the team in its move from Milwaukee, he hit five home runs and five doubles, driving in 23 runs. In 111 at bats, the North Carolina native recorded a respectable .234 average. Over his twelve-year major league career—which also included stops in Cincinnati and St. Louis—Cloninger hit .192 with 11 home runs in 621 at bats.

But two grand slams in a single game? Cloninger became the first National League player ever to accomplish the feat. For a pitcher, it was a surprising show of strength.

Christians have a similar power hidden deep within, an ability to handle hardship, resist temptation, give unselfishly, and succeed in all the most important areas of life. That power, of course, is our risen Savior, Jesus Christ. According to the apostle Paul in Philippians 4:13, "I can do all this through him who gives me strength."

Two grand slams and nine RBIs are an impressive sporting achievement. Christ in your life makes for success in the really important areas of life.

*God is our refuge and strength,*
*an ever-present help in trouble.*
PSALM 46:1

When the first "major league" game occurred on May 4, 1871, professional baseball began an unbroken string of seasons that stretches to this day.

On that occasion, the Fort Wayne Kekiongas shut out the Cleveland

**SEASONS**

Forest Citys 2–0, as Bobby Mathews picked up the first pitching victory in a National Association game. As that 1871 season progressed, the Kekiongas would fold, as would Cleveland's team the next year.

By 1876 the entire National Association was gone, replaced by a new "National League." Teams from Boston and Chicago moved from the National Association to the National League and continue in today's National League as the Braves and Cubs.

The American League burst onto the scene in 1901, with teams from Chicago, Boston, Detroit, Philadelphia, Baltimore, Washington, Cleveland, and Milwaukee (listed in order of their finish). With occasional additions, subtractions, and moving of teams, both the National and American Leagues have played uninterrupted baseball for more than a hundred seasons.

By definition, a season is a period of time, limited rather than permanent. And that's how the Bible describes the satisfaction we get from sin: "By faith Moses, when he was come to years, refused to be called the son of Pharaoh's daughter; choosing rather to suffer affliction with the people of God, than to enjoy the pleasures of sin for a season" (Hebrews 11:24–25 KJV).

Sin—hatred, laziness, lust, you name it—can "feel" good. But there's no future in it. When that season of pleasure tempts you, do what Moses did: "He regarded disgrace for the sake of Christ as of greater value than the treasures of Egypt, because he was looking ahead to his reward" (Hebrews 11:26).

*Surely goodness and love will follow me all the days of my life; and I will dwell in the house of the LORD forever.*
PSALM 23:6

The play was destined for highlight-film immortality.

It happened early in another forgettable season for the Cleveland Indians, who were on their way to a 76–86 record for 1993. Batting against the Rangers, who would finish second in the American League West with a mirror-image 86–76 mark, light-hitting utility man

## KEEP YOUR EYE ON THE BALL

Carlos Martinez got a good swing, driving the ball toward Texas right fielder Jose Canseco. The former Oakland A, once feared for his slugging, sprinted toward the right field wall to make one of the more amazing plays in baseball history.

It wasn't a catch.

Canseco got underneath the drive but lost focus as he made an awkward last-second turn. The ball dropped past Canseco's outstretched glove, bounced squarely off his head, and vaulted the wall for a home run. The Indians went on to win the game 7–6.

"Keep your eye on the ball" is one of the fundamentals of the game. The rule has a parallel in our Christian lives, as we see in Jesus' warning to a Peter wannabe.

"I will follow you, Lord," the would-be disciple said; "but first let me go back and say goodbye to my family" (Luke 9:61). Never satisfied with halfhearted commitment, Jesus responded with a farming image His followers could easily understand: "No one who puts a hand to the plow and looks back is fit for service in the kingdom of God" (Luke 9:62).

In other words: Always keep your eye on the goal. Bad things can happen when you lose your focus.

*... fixing our eyes on Jesus, the pioneer and perfecter of faith.*
*For the joy set before him he endured the cross, scorning its*
*shame, and sat down at the right hand of the throne of God.*
HEBREWS 12:2

# MARIANO RIVERA

**Born:** November 29, 1969
**Height:** 6' 2"
**Weight:** 185 pounds
**Throws:** Right
**Bats:** Right

**Quote:** "I wanted to study to be a mechanic. Obviously, I didn't do it because the Lord had different plans for me. I always have to talk about God, because that's the most important thing in my life. Yes, there have been bumps in the road, but God gave me the strength."

## MAJOR LEAGUE RECORD

*Signed:* amateur free agent by New York Yankees, 1990

*MLB debut:* May 23, 1995 (age 25), with New York Yankees

*Stat highlights:* 53 saves (2004), 1.38 ERA (2005), 130 strikeouts (1996)

Frank Hahn had a memorable nickname—"Noodles"—and an equally memorable six-year run as pitcher for the Cincinnati Reds. Hahn posted a 23–8 record in 1899, his rookie campaign, and averaged 20 wins a season for the next five years. He led the National League in strikeouts from 1899 to 1901, recorded a 1.77 earned run average in 1902, and by 1904 had amassed 122 victories. Noodles Hahn was hot.

## COLD NOODLES

But then Noodles went cold. From his league-leading 375⅓ innings pitched and personal best 42 games started in 1901, Hahn quickly sank into oblivion. In the 1905 and 1906 seasons, he appeared only briefly for the Reds and was soon out of the game completely. Frank "Noodles" Hahn was a has-been at age twenty-seven.

In life, as in baseball, there's little opportunity to rest on one's laurels. No matter how successful we were yesterday, there's always tomorrow—and like Noodles Hahn, we may find that all the successes of prior years won't carry us through the demands of today.

In a classic Bible passage, the apostle Paul addressed the issue of spiritual success when he wrote, "I do not consider myself yet to have taken hold of it [complete Christlikeness]. But one thing I do: Forgetting what is behind and straining toward what is ahead, I press on toward the goal to win the prize for which God has called me heavenward in Christ Jesus" (Philippians 3:13–14).

It's good to know that God isn't like a fickle fan or worried owner, turning on his "players" at their first signs of trouble. But in the Christian life, there's also no place for coasting—either you're moving forward or you're falling behind.

*Only let us live up to what we have already attained.*
PHILIPPIANS 3:16

Wins, losses, batting average, earned run average—many aspects of baseball can be measured accurately and with certainty. Those objective figures then provide ammunition for the subjective arguments fans enjoy, such as comparing players of different eras or selecting the best team of all time.

**WORST DRESSED**

Some judgments, though, have nothing to do with statistics, relying entirely on personal preference. Take, for example, the issue of ugly uniforms.

In late 2006, the CNN/*Sports Illustrated* website featured a photo gallery of its "Worst Dressed Teams in Sports." Among the sixteen professional uniforms spotlighted were three major league outfits. The winners (or losers, as the case may be)?

- the Devil Rays, with a modernistic teal "Tampa Bay" across their light gray jerseys
- the Atlanta Braves, sporting a bright orange jersey with blue piping and a large tomahawk logo across the chest
- the Mets, whose black jerseys featured orange and blue "New York" lettering in an 1890s style font

The Houston Astros and San Diego Padres of the 1970s can be thankful they weren't included in the CNN/SI survey. Whether for a yellow-, orange-, and red-striped jersey or a gold-and-brown combo, respectively, who wants to be known for unappealing attire?

The Bible's second-to-last book highlights an outfit worthy of actual loathing: "[hate] even the clothing stained by corrupted flesh" (Jude 23). That unusual command follows a positive appeal to "keep yourselves in God's love as you wait for the mercy of our Lord Jesus Christ to bring you to eternal life" (Jude 21).

The choices we make in life can land us on either a best- or worst-dressed list, spiritually speaking. Which will you choose today?

> *"I put on righteousness as my clothing;*
> *justice was my robe and my turban."*
>
> JOB 29:14

Bobby Thomson put the exclamation point on one of baseball's most amazing comebacks.

Late in the 1951 season, Thomson's New York Giants trailed their crosstown rivals, the Brooklyn Dodgers, by 13½ games in the National League pennant race. But on

## THE SHOT HEARD 'ROUND THE WORLD

August 12, New York began a 16-game winning streak to make the Dodgers sweat. By winning 39 of their final 47 games, including their last seven in a row, the Giants tied Brooklyn for first place, setting up a three-game playoff.

The teams split their first two games, and Brooklyn took the early advantage in Game 3. The Dodgers led 4–1 going into the bottom of the ninth when the Giants once again rallied. A pair of singles followed by a double cut the lead to 4–2, chasing Brooklyn pitcher Don Newcombe. Reliever Ralph Branca entered the game with two out, two on, and a two-run lead—but put his second pitch where Thomson could hit it. The resulting three-run home run electrified fans, propelled the Giants into the World Series, and earned baseball immortality as "the shot heard 'round the world."

Some nineteen hundred years earlier, Jesus' disciples delivered an infinitely more powerful jolt by spreading the good news of the Gospel. Even people who hated the message, like a jealous mob in Thessalonica, admitted its impact: "These that have turned the world upside down are come hither also" (Acts 17:6 KJV).

As Christians, we know the truth that can change our families, workplaces, communities, and nation for the better. Are you sharing it with others? The Gospel of Jesus Christ could be your own "shot heard 'round the world."

*"Let your light shine before others, that they may see your good deeds and glorify your Father in heaven."*
MATTHEW 5:16

Phil Rizzuto's career in baseball—as a player and broadcaster—spanned more than a half century. It even led to a new notation for scorekeepers.

The 5-foot, 6-inch shortstop nicknamed "Scooter" debuted with the

**WASN'T WATCHING**

Yankees in 1941, beginning a thirteen-year playing career followed by nearly four decades as a pinstripe announcer. Number 10 played on nine of New York's pennant-winning teams (taking seven World Series titles) and announced for several more championship clubs. In 1994, at the urging of baseball legend Ted Williams, the Veteran's Committee voted Rizzuto into baseball's Hall of Fame in Cooperstown, New York.

Well known for his folksy style and popular exclamation "Holy cow!" Rizzuto also coined a new scorecard notation in the broadcast booth. For the occasional missed play, Scooter would jot down "ww"—short for "wasn't watching."

A baseball announcer might get away with a "ww" now and then, but Jesus expects His followers always to be on alert:

- "Watch out that you are not deceived. For many will come in my name, claiming, 'I am he,' and, 'The time is near.' Do not follow them" (Luke 21:8).
- "Watch out! Be on your guard against all kinds of greed; life does not consist in an abundance of possessions" (Luke 12:15).
- "Watch and pray so that you will not fall into temptation. The spirit is willing, but the flesh is weak" (Mark 14:38).
- "Keep watch, because you do not know on what day your Lord will come" (Matthew 24:42).

We as Christians should always have our head in the game with one eye on our competition and the other on our leader. Let's never have to say to Jesus, "I wasn't watching."

*"What I say to you, I say to everyone: 'Watch!'"*
MARK 13:37

What was baseball's greatest era? For many, it's the years of their own youth.

Fans from the 1980s remember George Brett's .390 batting average, Nolan Ryan's record fifth no-hitter, Orel Hershiser's 67 consecutive shutout innings, and the debut of Roger Clemens. Then there were the '70s, the era of dynasties like the Oakland A's and Cincinnati's Big Red Machine, featuring

## THE GOOD OLD DAYS

Johnny Bench, Joe Morgan, and Pete Rose. In the '60s, Roger Maris chased Babe Ruth's single season home run record, Sandy Koufax dominated National League batters, Hank Aaron slammed 375 home runs, and Willie Mays made basket catches in center field.

For fans of the 1950s, there were Stan Musial, Mickey Mantle, Jackie Robinson, and Yogi Berra, while the '40s saw many of baseball's greatest stars serving the war effort. The 1930s are legendary for the Yankee teams of Lou Gehrig and Joe DiMaggio, while the Cubs' Hack Wilson was setting a single-season record of 190 RBIs. Of course, the Roaring '20s belonged to "the Bambino," George Herman Ruth.

Though they vary from fan to fan, "the good old days" are a time of superlative achievement never to be equaled or excelled. They have an honored place in baseball debate—but not the Christian life.

"Do not say, 'Why were the old days better than these?' " a biblical writer, thought by some to be Solomon, once wrote. "For it is not wise to ask such questions" (Ecclesiastes 7:10).

Why not? Because getting stuck in the past interferes with the present—and can jeopardize the future. Leave the "good old days" where they belong—in the past. God gives us today so we can work toward eternity.

*I lift up my eyes to you, to you who sit enthroned in heaven.*
PSALM 123:1

Sure, baseball is a big business. But it also creates childlike joy in many of its players.

While fans still debate Pete Rose's banishment from baseball, no one can question his enthusiasm for

**FOR LOVE OF THE GAME**

playing. The game's all-time hits leader was once quoted as saying, "I haven't missed a game in two and a half years. I go to the park as sick as a dog, and when I see my uniform hanging there, I get well right away." Another time, more colorfully, he said, "I'd walk through hell in a gasoline suit in order to play baseball."

Check out what other players said:

- "I am convinced that God wanted me to be a baseball player," said Pirates Hall of Famer Roberto Clemente, a member of the 3,000-hit club. "I was born to play baseball."
- Baltimore Hall of Famer Brooks Robinson called the game "a passion to the point of obsession," adding, "I'm a guy who just wanted to see his name in the lineup every day."
- Old-time pitcher Smokey Joe Wood, who played from 1908 to 1920, said, "Wherever I was I played baseball. That's all I lived for. When I sat up on the front seat of that covered wagon next to my father, I was wearing a baseball glove."

The thrill of playing baseball, though, should pale in comparison to our joy of living as Christians. With our past forgiven, our present secure, and our future settled, we as believers can savor life like no one else. According to the apostle Paul, "God . . . richly provides us with everything for our enjoyment" (1 Timothy 6:17).

Don't buy the idea that faith is somehow dour or dull. Your love of the game (of life) is actually an act of worship to God!

*"I [Jesus] have come that they may have life,*
*and have it to the full."*
JOHN 10:10

Pitcher Kyle Denney will never forget September 2004.

The Cleveland Indians rookie earned his first major league win, an 8–3 decision over the Royals on the 19th. Then, ten days later in Kansas City, he was shot in the leg while riding the team bus to the airport. Oh, and did we mention he was wearing a women's cheerleading outfit—complete with tall white boots—at the time?

**MEMORABLE**

The dress-up was part of a rookie hazing arranged by Tribe veterans. They selected a University of Southern California costume for Denney because his home-state Oklahoma Sooners were trailing the top-ranked Trojans in the college football polls.

As the Indians made a postgame ride to the airport on September 29, a random gunshot pierced the side of the team bus, lodging in Denney's right calf. Team trainers were able to remove the bullet on the scene—and credited the calf-high cheerleading boot for protecting the pitcher's leg from more serious damage.

It's a crazy way to be remembered—one that Kyle Denney certainly never sought out. We as Christians, though, have more control over what makes us memorable.

Do you want to be known as a good spouse or parent? For being ethical in your business dealings? For your generosity, compassion, or wisdom? If so, you'll need to make certain choices. Make the wrong decisions, and you'll be remembered in a very different way.

In a classic example of contrast, Proverbs 10:7 says, "The name of the righteous is used in blessings, but the name of the wicked will rot." Which way would you prefer?

*"Truly I tell you, wherever this gospel is preached throughout the world, what she has done will also be told, in memory of her."*
MATTHEW 26:13

Baseball has experienced its share of scandal—perhaps none bigger than the 1919 "Black Sox" affair.

When the Chicago White Sox lost a best-of-nine World Series to the Cincinnati Reds, five games to three, suspicion arose in baseball circles. Led by outfielder "Shoeless Joe" Jackson (fourth in American League batting at .351, third in runs batted in with 96) and pitchers Eddie Ciccotte (league-leading 29 wins, 1.82 ERA) and Lefty Williams (23 victories, 125 strikeouts, 2.64 ERA), the Sox were considered by many observers the team to beat. Chicago's loss led to rumors, investigations, and, the following season, the indictment of eight Sox players on charges of fixing the 1919 series.

**SAY IT AIN'T SO**

Though the "Black Sox" were acquitted at trial, new commissioner Kenesaw Mountain Landis, hoping to restore public trust in the game, barred them for life anyway. The scandal generated a catchphrase, supposedly aimed at Jackson by a distraught young fan: "Say it ain't so, Joe."

The Bible never addresses the issue of throwing sporting events for a cut of gambling profits—but it clearly warns against pursuing money by crooked means. "Am I still to forget," God said to corrupt Israel, "your ill-gotten treasures and the short ephah [a unit of measure], which is accursed? Shall I acquit someone with dishonest scales, with a bag of false weights?" (Micah 6:10–11).

Cheating in any form offends the Lord, who is the Truth (see John 14:6). If greed threatens to overwhelm your ethics, take a tip from baseball history and say, "It ain't so."

*A fortune made by a lying tongue is*
*a fleeting vapor and a deadly snare.*
PROVERBS 21:6

Question: What do Mark Koenig, Larry Haney, Cesar Geronimo, and Julio Lugo have in common? Answer: They were each lesser-known players on powerful World Series championship teams.

Koenig played for the 1927 Yankees in the shadow of superstars Babe Ruth and Lou Gehrig. The shortstop batted a respectable .285, smacking three home runs.

**TEAM SUCCESS**

Haney caught for the 1974 Oakland A's, the mighty dynasty of Reggie Jackson and Catfish Hunter. Clearly on the roster for his defense, Haney hit only .165.

Geronimo, a center fielder for the Big Red Machine, batted a healthy .307 in 1976, though teammates Pete Rose, Johnny Bench, and Joe Morgan got most of the press.

Lugo, a light-hitting shortstop for the 2007 Boston Red Sox, supported big-name stars like Manny Ramirez, David Ortiz, and Josh Beckett.

Though none of the four players was the biggest star on his team, each contributed to its success—and they all enjoyed the benefits of a World Series triumph.

Centuries ago, God told His people, the Jews, to contribute to the success of—can you believe this?—*Babylon,* which had overrun the nation of Judah and carried away its treasures as well as its most promising citizens as captives. Through the prophet Jeremiah, God urged those captives to "seek the peace and prosperity of the city to which I have carried you into exile. Pray to the LORD for it, because if it prospers, you too will prosper" (Jeremiah 29:7).

That principle, spoken some twenty-six hundred years ago, applies to us today—in our homes, our churches, our workplaces, and anywhere we interact with people.

In baseball, some win and others lose. But in God's economy, we can all succeed together. As you benefit others, you benefit yourself.

*A generous person will prosper; whoever*
*refreshes others will be refreshed.*
PROVERBS 11:25

To focus on Jimmie Foxx the hitter is to overlook Jimmie Foxx the whole player.

Certainly, the Hall of Famer was a master at the plate. In a two-decade career that began in 1925, Foxx blasted 534 home runs. He led the league in dingers four seasons, including 1932 when he hit 58 to challenge Babe Ruth's record of 60.

**ALL-AROUND GUY**

The man from Sudlersville, Maryland, also drove in prodigious numbers of runs: 1,922 for his career, including a league-best 175 in 1938. And Foxx hit for points as well as power—his lifetime batting average stands at .325.

But Jimmie Foxx was more than just a hitter. Overshadowed by his offensive record is the fact that Foxx could play most anywhere on defense—primarily first base, though over the course of his career he made an appearance at every position except second. On occasion, Foxx even pitched—throwing a perfect inning of relief in 1939, and then, in his final season, taking the mound nine times for the Philadelphia Phillies. He put on a good show: in 22⅔ innings pitched, 13 hits allowed, an earned run average of 1.59. Jimmie Foxx was truly an all-around guy.

Nearly two thousand years ago, the apostle Paul turned in an impressive all-around performance as he tried to point as many people as possible to Jesus: "To the Jews I became like a Jew, to win the Jews. To those under the law I became like one under the law. . . . To those not having the law I became like one not having the law. . . . To the weak I became weak, to win the weak. I have become all things to all people so that by all possible means I might save some" (1 Corinthians 9:20–22).

God is pleased with the "all-around guys" on His roster. How are you performing today?

*Whoever turns a sinner from the error of their way will save them from death and cover over a multitude of sins.*

JAMES 5:20

# CLAYTON KERSHAW

***Nickname:*** The Claw

**Quote:** "It's an overwhelming task because you can't get to every kid. It's hard. Some people don't go because you think, 'It's just one person.' But one kid you do help is one life affected."

## AWARDS AND HONORS

- All-Star 2011, 2012, 2013
- Cy Young Award 2011, 2013
- National League *The Sporting News* Pitcher of the Year 2011
- Gold Glove 2011
- Roberto Clemente Award 2012

## MINISTRIES

- Los Angeles Dodgers Baseball Chapel representative
- Arise Africa, addressing spiritual and physical poverty

Just as the British Invasion transformed the pop landscape in the 1960s, the Japanese infiltrated Major League Baseball a few decades later.

## FOREIGNERS AND STRANGERS

Players such as Hideo Nomo, Kazuhiro Sasaki, Ichiro Suzuki, and So Taguchi brought the skills they polished in Japan to North American baseball. In many cases, they made a quick and lasting impression.

Nomo went 13–6 for the Dodgers in 1995, helping his team to the playoffs, appearing in the All-Star Game, and winning the National League Rookie of the Year award. Sasaki and Suzuki nabbed the American League Rookie of the Year awards in 2000 and 2001, respectively, both with the Mariners. Sasaki notched 37 saves in his rookie campaign, while Suzuki had league-leading figures in hits (242) and batting average (.350) as a freshman. Taguchi's contributions weren't as immediate, but the fifth-year outfielder hit a dramatic postseason home run against the Mets to help his Cardinals toward the 2006 World Series title.

Even in today's ethnically integrated game of baseball, Japanese players still stand out. To borrow a biblical phrase, they're kind of "foreigners and strangers"—like the faith heroes of Hebrews 11.

"Admitting that they were foreigners and strangers on earth," is how the Bible describes God-pleasing people like Abel, Noah, and Abraham. "People who say such things show that they are looking for a country of their own. . . . They were longing for a better country—a heavenly one. Therefore God is not ashamed to be called their God, for he has prepared a city for them" (Hebrews 11:13–14, 16).

As Christians, we, too, should stand out from the world—as we look forward to the home in heaven God has prepared for us.

*Dear friends, I urge you, as foreigners and exiles, to abstain from sinful desires, which wage war against your soul.*
1 Peter 2:11

Some 200,000 games have occurred in the century-plus history of Major League Baseball. Only about 1 in 10,000 have been *perfect* games.

By definition, a perfect game is one in which the winning pitcher allows no hits, no runs, or opposing batters to reach base. Though many pitchers have achieved greatness, the perfect gamers are truly elite: at the time of this writing, twenty-three names appear on the list.

**THE ELITE**

Interestingly, the first two perfect games occurred within a week of each other, on June 12 and 17, 1880. Lee Richmond of the Worcester Brown Stockings threw the first; John M. Ward of the Providence Grays the second.

The great Cy Young, playing for the Red Sox, was the first pitcher of the modern era to hurl a perfecto on May 5, 1904. After that came Addie Joss (Cleveland, 1908); Charlie Robertson (White Sox, 1922); Don Larsen (Yankees, 1956—in the World Series!); Jim Bunning (Phillies, 1964); Sandy Koufax (Dodgers, 1965); Catfish Hunter (A's, 1968); Len Barker (Indians, 1981); Mike Witt (Angels, 1984); Tom Browning (Reds, 1988); Dennis Martinez (Expos, 1991); Kenny Rogers (Rangers, 1994); David Wells (Yankees, 1998); David Cone (Yankees, 1999); Randy Johnson (Diamondbacks, 2004); Mark Buehrle (White Sox, 2009); Dallas Braden (A's, 2010); Roy Halladay (Phillies, 2010); Phil Humber (White Sox, 2012); Matt Cain (Giants, 2012); and Felix Hernandez (Mariners, 2012). Notice that there were *three* perfect games in 2012, which was an anomaly.

Christians are part of an elite group, too—but not by virtue of our own great performances. One of Jesus' parables describes a king who invited a lot of people to his son's wedding banquet but found that many refused the offer. The story ends with the familiar quotation, "Many are invited, but few are chosen" (Matthew 22:14).

It's nice to be "elite"—but resist any urge to be elitist. When you find perfection—that free gift of salvation—be ready to share it.

*"Enter through the narrow gate. For wide is the gate and broad is the road that leads to destruction, and many enter through it. But small is the gate and narrow the road that leads to life, and only a few find it."*
MATTHEW 7:13–14

It had to feel like a dream for the St. Louis Browns' Bobo Holloman.

On May 6, 1953, the twenty-eight-year-old rookie threw a no-hitter in his first major league start. In shutting down the Philadelphia Athletics, "Bobo," born Alva Lee Holloman in Thomaston, Georgia, became the only pitcher in the twentieth century to accomplish that feat.

**BOBO'S NO-NO**

Bobo's dream, however, soon took on a nightmare hue. Shortly after his amazing debut, Holloman was sent back in the minors, where he recorded an earned run average over 5.00 with Toronto of the International League.

With the Browns in '53, Bobo would post a 3–7 record and a 5.23 ERA in 22 games. In 65⅓ innings, Holloman gave up 69 hits, 50 bases on balls, and 41 runs. The no-hitter would be the only complete game Bobo would ever pitch in the big leagues, in the only season he would ever appear in a major league uniform.

Bobo Holloman had a great start with a disappointing ending, the kind of thing the apostle Paul warned against in the spiritual realm. Though he knew nothing of baseball, Paul used many athletic analogies in his writings, like this one in 1 Corinthians 9:24: "Do you not know that in a race all the runners run, but only one gets the prize? Run in such a way as to get the prize."

In the Christian life, late failure overshadows early success. A strong ending is essential.

*The end of a matter is better than its beginning.*
ECCLESIASTES 7:8

Steady at the plate, sparkling in the field, loyal to his team—that combination carried Brooks Robinson to Cooperstown.

The man from Little Rock, Arkansas, led with his glove more than his bat. In 2,870 career games, all but 30 played at third base, Robinson was a defensive artist. In his twenty-three-year career, he led the league eleven times in fielding

**DEDICATION**

average and won sixteen consecutive Gold Glove awards from 1960 to 1975.

Robinson's offensive talents may have been a notch below his fielding prowess, but he still put up some solid numbers. In 1964 he led the league in runs batted in, recording 118. Six times Robinson smashed 20 or more home runs, finishing his playing days with 268 round trippers. In 1962 and again in '64, he batted over .300 (.303 and .317, respectively), posting a .267 average for his career.

And then there was Brooks Robinson's loyalty to his team. The Hall of Famer played his entire career—from his 1955 rookie season to his swan song in 1977—with the Baltimore Orioles. Now that's twenty-two years of dedication.

Jesus expects a similar commitment from us—that we make the most of the skills He has given us, and that we readily associate with our "team." Free agency, you see, is not an option in the Christian life. "Whoever acknowledges me before others, I will also acknowledge before my Father in heaven," Jesus said. "But whoever disowns me before others, I will disown before my Father in heaven" (Matthew 10:32–33).

If you're ever tempted to hide your faith, think of Brooks Robinson—and stay the course. Loyalty wins in the end.

*If you declare with your mouth, "Jesus is Lord," and believe in your heart that God raised him from the dead, you will be saved.*
ROMANS 10:9

The numbers added up in La Marr Hoyt's fifth season.

The Columbia, South Carolina, native played only eight years in the major leagues but enjoyed some notable successes on the mound. As a late-season call-up of the White Sox in 1979, Hoyt appeared in just two games, giving up two hits and no earned runs in three innings of work. Then in each of the next two seasons, he went 9–3 for the Pale Hose.

**NUMBERS ON YOUR SIDE**

The win total jumped to a league-leading 19 in the '82 campaign, a preview of Hoyt's career season to come. In 1983 the 6-foot, 1-inch right-hander won a league-high 24 games against only 10 losses for a .706 winning percentage. He led the White Sox to their first-ever American League West divisional crown and pitched Chicago's only victory in the American League Championship Series against Baltimore. After the season, he was named the Cy Young Award winner.

Key to Hoyt's success was keeping runners off the base paths: in 1983, he yielded only 1.07 walks per game, held opponents to a .238 batting average, and posted a league-low opponents' on-base percentage of .260. With numbers like those, how could he not succeed?

Christians, too, have "numbers" on their side. Remember the prophet Elisha encouraging his fearful servant with the words, "Don't be afraid. . . . Those who are with us are more than those who are with them" (2 Kings 6:16)? At that point, the servant could see past the enemy army to note "the hills full of horses and chariots of fire" (2 Kings 6:17).

It's been said that "God plus you equals the majority." If you're a believer, the numbers are always on your side.

> *You, dear children, are from God and have overcome*
> *[the antichrist spirits], because the one who is in*
> *you is greater than the one who is in the world.*
>
> 1 JOHN 4:4

The majors soared a mile high in 1993.

That's the year the Colorado Rockies entered the National League. Half of an expansion that also included the Florida Marlins, Colorado fielded a team highlighted by first baseman Andrés Galarraga (All-Star selection, league-leading .370 batting average), third baseman Charlie Hayes (.305 batting

## LOOKING UP

average, league-leading 45 doubles), and right fielder Dante Bichette (.310 batting average, 21 home runs, 43 doubles). The Don Baylor–managed Rockies finished 67–95, sixth out of seven teams in the National League West.

Colorado fans came out in droves, with the Rockies welcoming a record 4.4 million fans for their first campaign. The faithful would be rewarded with a postseason appearance only two years later, when wild card Colorado became the youngest expansion team ever to reach the playoffs. Playing in Denver's new Coors Field, the Rockies—also known as the Blake Street Bombers—boasted four hitters with at least 30 home runs: Bichette (40), Larry Walker (36), Vinny Castilla (32), and Galarraga (31). That powerful offense was helped, in part, by the high altitude and thin air of the Mile High City.

Three thousand years earlier, a biblical writer sought help from the higher elevations. What did he find? That the power he needed was more spiritual than physical: "I lift up my eyes to the mountains—where does my help come from? My help comes from the LORD, the Maker of heaven and earth" (Psalm 121:1–2).

When you need help, look to the mountains (Rocky or otherwise)—only if they remind you of God the Creator. He's the only one strong enough, wise enough, and good enough to provide the assistance you need.

*Your righteousness is like the highest mountains,*
*your justice like the great deep.*
PSALM 36:6

Baseball lore is packed with memorable names—but not all of them belong to players.

Vin Scully, Ernie Harwell, Harry Caray, Jack Buck, and Mel Allen are among the elite *announcers* of the game, those

**BROADCASTING**

radio and television wizards who colorfully describe the play-by-play to untold millions of people beyond the ballpark walls.

Today the relationship between baseball and broadcasting is a fact of life. But on August 5, 1921, when Pittsburgh radio station KDKA first aired a match-up between the hometown Pirates and the Philadelphia Phillies, it was something for the record books. In that broadcast, the announcer did not describe the game as it transpired before his eyes. Instead, he "recreated" the game by reading play-by-play accounts from a newswire in the studio.

In time, of course, broadcasters earned an exalted spot in the ballparks. From Allen's "How about that!" to Caray's "Holy cow!" to Russ Hodges' exuberant "The Giants win the pennant! The Giants win the pennant!" following Bobby Thomson's 1951 "Shot Heard 'Round the World," baseball announcers have shared the excitement of the game with anyone willing to listen.

With a far more important message to share, shouldn't we as Christians be passing along the "play-by-play" to the good news of Jesus Christ? Remember the Lord's last recorded words on earth, after His resurrection and before His ascension to heaven? "You will be my witnesses in Jerusalem, and in all Judea and Samaria, and to the ends of the earth" (Acts 1:8).

Now that's broadcasting with a real purpose.

> *"I tell you, open your eyes and look at the fields!*
> *They are ripe for harvest."*
> JOHN 4:35

Did Babe Ruth really "call the shot" on his last World Series home run?

Baseball scholars still debate the story, with some assigning it to the category of legend. What we know for sure is that the Bambino, in the fifth inning of Game 3 of the 1932 Fall Classic, slammed a home run to the center field seats. The blast propelled New York to a 7–5 victory and ultimately a series sweep of the Cubs.

## THE CALLED SHOT

What's unclear is the meaning of a gesture Ruth made during the at bat. After the second strike, just before the home run, Ruth pointed toward the playing field, either at Chicago pitcher Charlie Root or perhaps past him, to the center field fence. Root rejected the idea of Ruth "calling" a home run, saying if the Babe had been so bold, "I'd have put one in his ear." Lou Gehrig, though, waiting on deck, insisted the gesture was a prediction of a coming round tripper. The Iron Horse spoke admiringly of his teammate's nerve—"calling his shot and getting away with it!"

Truth, fable, or something in between, the story is a classic of baseball lore. The idea of "calling our shots" appeals to us—we like to think of ourselves as being in control. It's an attractive concept, though not particularly biblical.

Some six hundred years before Christ, the prophet Jeremiah wrote, "LORD, I know that people's lives are not their own; it is not for them to direct their steps" (Jeremiah 10:23). Some three centuries before that, the wise King Solomon was penning a similar message: "In their hearts humans plan their course, but the LORD establishes their steps" (Proverbs 16:9).

Knowing that God is in control can limit the stress in our lives. It's actually liberating *not* to call our own shots.

*"I am the vine; you are the branches. If you remain in me and I in you, you will bear much fruit; apart from me you can do nothing."*
JOHN 15:5

Most players break into the majors in their twenties. A few get called up in their late teens. Then there was Joe Nuxhall.

**YOUNGSTERS**

Born in the Cincinnati area in 1928, Nuxhall pitched for his hometown Reds on June 10, 1944, seven weeks shy of his sixteenth birthday. In other words, he was *fifteen*!

The southpaw's debut was inauspicious—he gave up two hits, five walks, and five runs in just two-thirds of an inning, posting an earned run average of 67.50. That shelling would represent Nuxhall's only major league appearance until 1952, when the twenty-three-year-old pitcher began a fifteen-year career primarily in Cincinnati, but also briefly with the Kansas City Athletics and Los Angeles Angels.

A quirk of history provided Nuxhall's opportunity to become the youngest major league player of the twentieth century. With World War II at its height and many major league stars serving in the armed forces, baseball teams were scrambling to fill their rosters. Cincinnati turned to a player too young for the military—and, apparently, a little too young for big league baseball.

Youth has its advantages and disadvantages. It is characterized by energy and enthusiasm, but also by lack of experience. An Old Testament writer urged his readers, "Remember your Creator in the days of your youth, before the days of trouble come" (Ecclesiastes 12:1). A New Testament writer added, "Don't let anyone look down on you because you are young, but set an example for the believers in speech, in conduct, in love, in faith and in purity" (1 Timothy 4:12).

Are you young today? Seek maturity by focusing on God's will. Not so young today? Find a young person with whom you can share your wisdom.

*How can a young person stay on the path of purity?*
*By living according to your word.*
PSALM 119:9

The St. Louis Browns were never a great team. But on June 8, 1950, they were downright awful.

In a game at Boston, the Browns—who in 1954 became the Baltimore Orioles—gave up 29 runs to the Red Sox. The Beantown Boys pushed across eight runs in the second inning, five in the third, and seven more in the fourth to make the score 20–3 going into the fifth. In that inning, St. Louis pitchers gave up two more runs then held Boston scoreless in the sixth. But a pair of runs in the seventh and five more in the eighth gave the Red Sox a record total of 29. Had Boston batted again in the bottom of the ninth, who knows what the final score might have been?

**WIPED OUT**

For the perennially weak Browns—on their way to a second-to-last-place finish, 40 games behind pennant-winning New York—the June 8 wipeout was the most dramatic event in a long history of embarrassing disappointments. But there would be no quitting. With some three months remaining in the season, St. Louis had to pick up the pieces and press on.

The apostle Peter faced a similar necessity after denying three times that he even *knew* his friend and Lord, Jesus Christ. But Jesus had already planned for Peter's restoration, as He said on the night of the Last Supper: "Simon, Simon, Satan has asked to sift all of you as wheat. But I have prayed for you, Simon, that your faith may not fail. And when you have turned back, strengthen your brothers" (Luke 22:31–32).

Since we're all human, failure, embarrassment, even occasional wipe-outs will occur in our lives. If you're part of God's family, though, there's always the promise of a better day ahead.

*"Repent, then, and turn to God, so that your sins may be wiped out, that times of refreshing may come from the Lord."*
ACTS 3:19

# ALBERT PUJOLS

**Nickname:** Prince Albert, The Machine

**Quote:** "One thing I have learned is that it's not about me; it's about serving the Lord Jesus Christ."

## AWARDS AND HONORS

- All-Star 2001, 2003, 2004, 2005, 2006, 2007, 2008, 2009, 2010
- National League Rookie of the Year 2001
- Major League Player of the Year (*The Sporting News*) 2003, 2008, 2009
- National League MVP 2005, 2008, 2009
- Gold Glove 2006, 2010
- Silver Slugger 2001, 2003, 2004, 2008, 2009, 2010
- Hank Aaron Award 2003, 2009
- Lou Gehrig Memorial Award 2009
- Roberto Clemente Award 2008

## MINISTRIES

- The Pujols Family Foundation, strengthening families with Down syndrome children and improving the lives of the impoverished in the Dominican Republic

To be traded is nothing unusual. But Joel Youngblood's experience stands as unique.

Primarily an outfielder over fourteen major league seasons, Youngblood came up with the Cincinnati Reds in 1976 then began the next year with the St. Louis Cardinals. Partway through the '77 campaign, Youngblood joined the

**TRADING PLACES**

New York Mets, for whom he played the next four full seasons, earning an All-Star berth in 1981.

With the Mets in 1982, however, Youngblood secured a spot in the history books. On August 4, during an afternoon game in Chicago, Youngblood learned he had been traded to the Expos. One inning after breaking a 1–1 tie with a bases-loaded single, he was packing bags for a flight to Philadelphia, where he would join his new club. Arriving at the stadium in the third, Youngblood watched from the dugout for three innings until Montreal manager Jim Fanning called him to replace outfielder Jerry White. In his only at bat that evening, Youngblood singled off Steve Carlton, becoming the first player ever to get a hit for two different teams, in two cities, on the same day.

For the Houston native, it was an amazing turnaround—but nothing like the one awaiting us as Christians. A day will come when every believer leaves this earth to be transported immediately into God's presence. As the apostle Paul told the church at Corinth, "As long as we are at home in the body we are away from the Lord. . . . We are confident, I say, and would prefer to be away from the body and at home with the Lord" (2 Corinthians 5:6, 8).

For Christians, trading places means perfection. Isn't that exciting?

*"If I go and prepare a place for you, I will come back and take you to be with me that you also may be where I am."*
JOHN 14:3

The Brooklyn Dodgers always seemed a poor stepsister to the crosstown New York Giants.

From 1890 through 1957, the Big Apple sported two National League

**SWEET REVENGE**

teams. During the early years, the Giants were generally more successful, winning thirteen pennants and four World Series through 1937. Brooklyn, on the other hand, won only four pennants and no World Series during the same period. It was even a struggle to name the team—Brooklyn called its players the Grays, Bridegrooms, Superbas, and Robins before settling on Dodgers, a shortened form of Trolley-Dodgers.

In 1933 Brooklyn finished in sixth place, 26½ games behind the pennant-winning Giants, who went on to win the World Series four games to one over the Washington Senators. As the 1934 campaign began, Giants' manager Bill Terry, asked to comment on the Dodgers' outlook, answered, "Is Brooklyn still in the league?"

That bit of disrespect would come back to haunt the New York manager. The Dodgers defeated Terry's Giants in the final two games of the season, knocking them out of pennant contention and giving the flag to the St. Louis Cardinals.

While revenge can be sweet in the baseball standings, there's no place for it in the Christian life. The apostle Paul wrote, "Do not take revenge, my dear friends, but leave room for God's wrath, for it is written: 'It is mine to avenge; I will repay,' says the Lord" (Romans 12:19).

"Sweet revenge" can become very bitter in your life. Leave that job to God.

> *If your enemy is hungry, give him food to eat; if he is thirsty, give him water to drink. In doing this, you will heap burning coals on his head, and the LORD will reward you.*
> PROVERBS 25:21–22

Today's baseball fans might find it hard to imagine a nonintegrated game.

For decades, many of baseball's greatest stars have been black: home run masters Hank Aaron, Willie Mays, and Barry Bonds; speedy base stealers Rickey Henderson and Lou Brock; pitching whizzes Satchel Paige, Bob Gibson, and Ferguson Jenkins. But for the first half of the twentieth century, the major leagues had a KEEP OUT sign for African-American players.

# THE COLOR LINE

Things changed—dramatically—in 1947, when Brooklyn Dodgers general manager Branch Rickey defied the racist tradition. Rickey brought on a talented black player named Jackie Robinson, positioning him at first base. Facing indifference or harassment from fans, opposing players, and even his own teammates, the twenty-eight-year-old turned in a Rookie of the Year season—playing in 151 games, batting .297 with a dozen home runs, and stealing a league-leading 29 bases. Robinson's efforts helped the Dodgers win the National League pennant for the first time in six years.

By breaking the so-called "color line," Jackie Robinson blazed a trail for other black players to follow: Larry Doby later that season with the Indians, and hundreds more to follow. By welcoming every talented player—regardless of background—baseball became a better game.

As Christians, we should welcome every fellow believer, regardless of his or her background or skin color. The apostle Paul, writing to the church in Colossae, said, "Here there is no Gentile or Jew, circumcised or uncircumcised, barbarian, Scythian, slave or free, but Christ is all, and is in all" (Colossians 3:11).

When we live up to that truth, we're all better people.

*There is no difference between Jew and Gentile—the same Lord is Lord of all and richly blesses all who call on him.*
ROMANS 10:12

Some guys can't seem to catch a break.

For ten of his sixteen major league seasons, pitcher Juan Marichal was superb. From 1962 through 1971, the San Francisco right-hander earned nine All-Star selections, winning 202 games. Twenty-win seasons were the 6-foot Dominican's specialty—he won at least 20 games six times, and 25 or more games in three of those seasons: 1963, when his 25 wins and 321⅓ innings pitched both led the National League; 1966, when his 25–6 record generated a league-topping .806 winning percentage; and 1968, when his 26 wins, 30 complete games, and 326 innings pitched were all league highs.

**WHAT ABOUT ME?**

And how many Cy Young Awards did Marichal win? Not one.

Marichal, you see, was privileged to throw against some of baseball's greatest pitchers ever—the Dodgers' Sandy Koufax, who won the Cy Young three times during Marichal's career; the Cardinals' Bob Gibson, who was honored twice; and other greats like Don Drysdale and Tom Seaver. Marichal was very good—but other pitchers always seemed to beat him out.

That happens even in the Christian life. We try to be good, honoring the Lord in our personal behavior, our families, and our work, but it's the "other guys"—often, those who ignore or even mock God—who seem to win. They have more money, better health, seemingly smoother lives. Even the psalm writer Asaph struggled with the unfairness of it all: "I envied the arrogant when I saw the prosperity of the wicked" (Psalm 73:3). But later, when he entered God's sanctuary, Asaph said, "then I understood their final destiny" (see Psalm 73:16–17).

Just something to consider when you're tempted to ask, "What about me?"

> But as for me, it is good to be near God. I have made the
> Sovereign LORD my refuge; I will tell of all your deeds.
> PSALM 73:28

For every slugger who socks 50 homers in a season, there are several guys for whom that would make a nice career. Or several careers.

Consider Sandy Alomar, Sr., a middle infielder for the Brewers, Braves, Mets, White Sox, Angels, Yankees, and Rangers from 1964 to 1978. In those fifteen seasons, over 1,481 games and 4,760 at bats, Alomar—the father of major leaguers Sandy Jr. and Roberto—recorded 13 home runs.

**SUPERHUMAN POWER**

Felix Fermin patrolled the middle infield for the Pirates, Indians, Mariners, and Cubs from 1987 to 1996. His ten-year major league career included 903 games, 2,767 at bats, and four round trippers.

Over seventeen years (1982–1998), playing shortstop and second base for the Pirates and Braves, Rafael Belliard had 2,301 at bats in 1,155 games and swatted two homers.

And then there was Duane Kuiper, a twelve-year second baseman for Cleveland and San Francisco. He played in 1,057 games, recorded 3,379 at bats—and finished with exactly one home run.

For many players, the power of a Babe Ruth, a Hank Aaron, or a Chris Davis must seem positively superhuman. And it's only that kind of power that allows us as Christians to battle the schemes of our mighty enemy, Satan. We can "resist him," as 1 Peter 5:9 says, only by "standing firm in the faith."

What faith? "The gospel I preached to you," the apostle Paul wrote, "which you received and on which you have taken your stand" (1 Corinthians 15:1).

You can base a season—and a whole career—on that.

*For what I received I passed on to you as of first importance:*
*that Christ died for our sins according to the Scriptures, that he was*
*buried, that he was raised on the third day according to the Scriptures.*
1 CORINTHIANS 15:3–4

Three innings pitched, one strikeout, one hit, no runs allowed—not a bad outing for a major league reliever. A very impressive outing, though, for a *fifty-nine*-year-old pitcher throwing against batters half to a third his age.

**OLD-TIMERS GAME**

The great Satchel Paige wrapped up his baseball career on September 25, 1965, with a relief appearance for the Kansas City Athletics. Just one year shy of his sixtieth birthday, the future Hall of Famer set the mark as the oldest hurler in major league history.

Perhaps the opposing Red Sox batters scoffed at facing an "old-timer"—a man who began in the Negro League nearly forty years earlier. Maybe those same Boston boys returned to the dugout with a greater appreciation of the accumulated knowledge and wisdom of the elderly.

"Gray hair," according to the Bible, "is a crown of splendor; it is attained in the way of righteousness" (Proverbs 16:31). We all know older Christians, whether relatives, neighbors, coworkers, or fellow church members, who have lived that righteous life.

What might you learn today from those old-timers? They've likely experienced, at one time or another, whatever issue you're dealing with now, and they can probably offer some helpful insights well worth considering.

If you're one of those old-timers yourself, why not seek out ways to help a younger person struggling with some trial in life? On God's "team," wisdom is always to be respected and shared.

> *"Stand up in the presence of the aged, show respect for the elderly and revere your God. I am the LORD."*
> LEVITICUS 19:32

Modern fans may find it hard to believe, but there was a time when darkness regularly interfered with major league games.

Though amateur and minor league teams had at times experimented with night baseball, the major leagues were slow to adopt artificial illumination. Cincinnati, which fielded the first openly professional baseball team in 1869,

**LET THERE BE LIGHT**

became the big leagues' night game pioneer sixty-six years later. The first game under the lights happened when the Reds defeated Philadelphia 2–1 at Crosley Field on May 24, 1935.

When Brooklyn became the majors' second team to install stadium lights, the Reds were the first opponent. The June 15, 1938, game at Ebbets Field took on even greater historical significance when Cincinnati pitcher Johnny Vander Meer, coming off a no-hitter against the Boston Braves, held the Dodgers hitless in winning 6–0. To this point, Vander Meer is the only pitcher to throw consecutive no-hitters.

Fifty years would pass before baseball's final day-game holdouts, the Chicago Cubs, installed lights. The Cubs would defeat the New York Mets 6–4 in the first official Wrigley Field night game, August 9, 1988.

You need light, of course, to play baseball. And you need light, spiritually speaking, to make your way through life successfully. Where do you find that kind of light? Only in the Bible: "We also have the prophetic message as something completely reliable, and you will do well to pay attention to it, as to a light shining in a dark place, until the day dawns and the morning star rises in your hearts" (2 Peter 1:19).

Until we're actually in the presence of Jesus, the Word Himself (John 1:1), we should regularly be in His written Word, the Bible. You don't want the darkness interfering with your "game."

*Your word is a lamp for my feet, a light on my path.*
PSALM 119:105

Hypothetical match-ups we'd love to see:

- Famed slugger Babe Ruth (714 home runs, .342 lifetime batting average) versus modern fireballers Roger Clemens (4,604 strikeouts), Randy Johnson (4,581 strikeouts), or Nolan Ryan (5,714 strikeouts, 321 home runs allowed over twenty-seven years).

**WHO'D GET BRAGGING RIGHTS?**

- Home run hitters like Hank Aaron (755) and Willie Mays (660) against early pitching stars Cy Young (511 career wins, 2.63 ERA), Walter Johnson (417 career wins, 3,509 strikeouts, 2.17 ERA), and Christy Mathewson (373 career wins, 2.13 ERA).
- A single-season stolen base contest featuring Ty Cobb (897 in twenty-four seasons), Lou Brock (938 in nineteen seasons), and Rickey Henderson (1,406 in twenty-five seasons).

So who'd win these mammoth match-ups? Considering all the variables, it's impossible to say.

It would be like debating who's the greatest Christian. Judge for yourself from this story Jesus told: "Two men went up to the temple to pray, one a Pharisee and the other a tax collector. The Pharisee stood by himself and prayed: 'God, I thank you that I am not like other people—robbers, evildoers, adulterers—or even like this tax collector. I fast twice a week and give a tenth of all I get.' But the tax collector stood at a distance. He would not even look up to heaven, but beat his breast and said, 'God, have mercy on me, a sinner.' I tell you that this man, rather than the other, went home justified before God. For all those who exalt themselves will be humbled, and those who humble themselves will be exalted" (Luke 18:10–14).

Debating who's a better player is an enjoyable pastime. Judging ourselves better than others is just dangerous.

*We do not dare to classify or compare ourselves with some who commend themselves. When they measure themselves by themselves and compare themselves with themselves, they are not wise.*

2 CORINTHIANS 10:12

You'd think that a team winning 103 games would be a shoo-in for the postseason. Not in 1954.

A powerful Yankees team began that season seeking its sixth straight American League championship. From 1949 through 1953, New York hogged the pennant, winning between 95 and 99 games a season. In 1954, as the only team

## NOT GOOD ENOUGH

in the majors to score more than 800 runs, the Yankees upped their win total to 103—and finished second by *eight* full games.

The Cleveland Indians, who'd won the World Series the season before the Yankees' pennant string began, put it all together again in '54. The Tribe's solid offense featured a trio of All-Stars—batting champion Bobby Avila (.341 average), home run and RBI leader Larry Doby (32 and 126, respectively), and Al Rosen (.300 average, 24 home runs)—while its pitching crew was one of the greatest of all time. Bob Lemon, Mike Garcia, Early Winn, and Bob Feller headlined a staff that gave up only 2.78 earned runs per game.

The '54 Yankees—awfully good, yet not good enough—bring to mind a comment in Jesus' Sermon on the Mount. Telling the crowds that He'd come not to abolish the Old Testament law but to fulfill it, Jesus said, "I tell you that unless your righteousness surpasses that of the Pharisees and the teachers of the law [well-known for their picky adherence to religious and ceremonial rules], you will certainly not enter the kingdom of heaven" (Matthew 5:20).

It was hard for the average person to be "more righteous" than the Pharisees and teachers of the law who, in reality, could never attain God's standard of holiness themselves. Nobody's good enough—that's why Jesus came.

*But now apart from the law the righteousness of God has been made known, to which the Law and the Prophets testify. This righteousness is given through faith in Jesus Christ to all who believe.*
Romans 3:21–22

What a difference a decade makes.

In 1911 Philadelphia Athletics third baseman Frank Baker began a four-year reign as American League home run champion. Baker swatted 11 dingers in 1911, 10 the next season, a career-high 12 in 1913, and 9 the following year.

**TALE OF TWO SLUGGERS**

After blasting two key home runs in the 1911 World Series, the man from Trappe, Maryland, earned a new moniker: he was no longer Frank Baker but "Home Run" Baker.

Ten years after his World Series heroics, now wearing Yankee pinstripes, "Home Run" Baker was teammate of a twenty-six-year-old fellow Marylander named George Herman Ruth. "Babe," as he was known, won the 1921 American League home run crown with 59 blasts, 17 more than Baker's league-leading totals from 1911 to 1914 *combined*. Who would have guessed that "Home Run's" efforts would be surpassed so dramatically?

Jesus once told His disciples that their accomplishments would eclipse even His own. After explaining that His miracles proved His connection to God the Father, Jesus said, "Very truly I tell you, whoever believes in me will do the works I have been doing, and they will do even greater things than these, because I am going to the Father" (John 14:12).

How could that be? Because, Jesus continued, the disciples would soon receive "the Holy Spirit, whom the Father will send in my name" (John 14:26). That power, unleashed at Pentecost, "turned the world upside down" (Acts 17:6 KJV).

It's a power we as Christians still have today.

> "This is the word of the LORD to Zerubbabel: 'Not by might nor by power, but by my Spirit,' says the LORD Almighty."
> ZECHARIAH 4:6

# ADRIAN GONZALEZ

***Nickname:*** A-Gon, Gonzo

**Quote:** "God has put me in a situation where I have a big platform to profess Christ to people, so I've got to take advantage. He's given me abilities to play this game, and I'm grateful for that. I do the best I can with them, and in return, try to be the best disciple I can for Him."

## AWARDS AND HONORS

- All-Star 2008, 2009, 2010, 2011
- Gold Glove 2008, 2009, 2011
- Silver Slugger 2011
- Silver Slugger 2011
- San Diego Padres MVP 2006, 2008, 2009, 2010

## MINISTRIES

- Team Bible study leader
- Faith Night organizer
- Habitat for Humanity
- Adrian & Betsy Gonzalez Foundation, assisting underprivileged youth

Long before Babe Ruth came along, there was Ned Williamson.

A third baseman with the Chicago White Stockings (the team we now know as the Cubs), Williamson established the pre-Ruth, single-season home run record, knocking 27 round trippers in 1884.

## QUESTIONABLE PERFORMANCE

In an era of low home run output, Williamson's record really stands out. His 1884 figure, in fact, is nearly one-fifth that of the *eighteen-year* total of the nineteenth century's home run king, Roger Connor. He notched 138 homers from 1880 to1897.

So why do some baseball historians pooh-pooh Williamson's feat?

Skeptics note that Chicago's home field that year, Lake Front Park, was very small, with a right field fence less than 200 feet from home plate. Williamson hit all but two of his 27 home runs at Lake Front—and the other two in the league's next smallest park in Buffalo. Besides that, three of Williamson's Chicago teammates also had big numbers in 1884, hitting 25, 22, and 21 home runs. When the White Stockings moved to a bigger park the following year, Williamson's home run total dropped to just four. In some historians' minds, Williamson's performance has a bad smell.

Questionable performances can occur in our Christian lives, too. If we cut ethical corners or crowd our moral boundaries, we risk tainting our own reputations and the testimony we share with the world. That's why the apostle Paul told the church at Ephesus, "But among you there must not be even a hint of sexual immorality, or of any kind of impurity, or of greed, because these are improper for God's holy people" (Ephesians 5:3).

> · You ought to live holy and godly lives as you look
> forward to the day of God and speed its coming.
> 2 PETER 3:11–12

Successful managers weren't always successful players. Just ask Sparky Anderson.

As a second baseman with the Philadelphia Phillies, the South Dakota native played only one year in the major leagues. Anderson finished that 1959 season—and his career—with a respectable .984 fielding percentage in 152 games. His

## TRUE CALLING

performance at the plate, however, was less than thrilling: 104 hits in 477 at bats for an average of only .218. And Anderson's total base count of 119 (he had nine doubles and three triples among his hit total) was one of the lowest ever for a full-time position player.

In his second career as a major league manager, however, Sparky caught fire. He took two of his first three teams, the 1970 and 1972 Cincinnati Reds, to the World Series. Though they lost each time (to the Orioles and A's, respectively), Sparky's team, as "The Big Red Machine," would be back to win the Big Show in both 1975 and '76.

In 1979 Anderson took over the Detroit Tigers, leading the Motown boys to a World Series title in 1984. In twenty-six years of managing, Anderson suffered only six losing seasons. He had, it seemed, found a much higher calling in the dugout.

Christians have a calling that exceeds all others. We should heed the call Jesus gave to the brothers Simon and Andrew, "Come, follow me." Why? So we, like those ancient Galileans, can "fish for people" (Mark 1:17) and point others to the Lord.

To represent Christ goes far beyond any pursuits in sports, business, hobbies, or other endeavors of life. Are you living up to your true calling today?

*All this is from God, who reconciled us to himself through*
*Christ and gave us the ministry of reconciliation....*
*We are therefore Christ's ambassadors.*
2 CORINTHIANS 5:18, 20

Ever hear of Eddie Robinson? How could you have missed him?

Throughout a thirteen-year major league career, it seemed Robinson was everywhere—at least in the American League. The first baseman debuted with Cleveland in 1942, getting one hit and two RBIs in eight at bats. Then he left baseball for three years to serve in World War II.

**TRAVELIN' MAN**

Robinson was back with the Tribe from 1946 to 1948, helping the Indians to a World Series title in his final season. From there he moved on to Washington, where he became an All-Star selection in 1949. Early the next year, Robinson joined the Chicago White Sox, where he was an All-Star in both 1951 (while hitting 29 home runs) and 1952. Another All-Star season, with the Philadelphia Athletics, followed; then he was off to the Yankees for more than two years.

Partway into the '56 campaign, Robinson became a Kansas City Athletic, and then, in his final season, 1957, split his time among Detroit, Cleveland (again), and Baltimore. Only one American League team of his day, Boston, never made use of Eddie Robinson's services.

"Travelin' man" well describes Eddie Robinson, the baseball player . . . as well as Abram, the Bible hero. Remember God's call in Genesis 12:1? "Go from your country, your people and your father's household to the land I will show you." The man from Ur stepped out in faith, and the rest is history—God blessed Abram in amazing ways, just as He had promised.

Where is God calling you today? Whether it's to a new land, a new task, or a new attitude, be ready to go.

*"Therefore go and make disciples of all nations, baptizing them in the name of the Father and of the Son and of the Holy Spirit."*
MATTHEW 28:19

The statistics tell the story of Jim Palmer's success.

Over a nineteen-year career played entirely with the Baltimore Orioles, Palmer won 268 games and lost only 152 for a winning percentage of .638. For three straight years, 1975–77, he led the American League in victories, with 23, 22, and 20, respectively; they were among eight seasons in which Palmer won 20 or more. Ten times he posted an earned run average under 3.00, besting all other American League hurlers in 1973 (2.40) and 1975 (2.09). After nearly two decades of pitching, Palmer retired with a sparkling ERA of 2.86.

**PROTECTED**

One of Palmer's most interesting accomplishments doesn't appear in most statistical tables—but it is cast in bronze on his plaque at the Baseball Hall of Fame: "Impressive numbers include . . . no grand slams allowed over entire 19-year career." In 558 career games, over 3,948 innings pitched, Jim Palmer never let the grand slam hurt him. His careful pitching protected him from a potentially disastrous swing of the bat.

We as Christians need to protect ourselves from the disastrous plans of Satan, who wants nothing more than to see us fall into sin. The apostle Paul suggested a few common trouble spots and offered advice on avoiding them: "Each of you must put off falsehood and speak truthfully to your neighbor, for we are all members of one body. 'In your anger do not sin': do not let the sun go down while you are still angry, and do not give the devil a foothold" (Ephesians 4:25–27).

How can you protect yourself against Satan's attacks? Always approach him very carefully.

*Put on the full armor of God so that you can take your stand against the devil's schemes.*
EPHESIANS 6:11

Who would guess that a lifetime .224 hitter, averaging one strikeout every 3.74 at bats, would be part of an elite group of offensive performers?

"Unremarkable" certainly describes Pat Seerey's major league career.

**PAT'S BAT**

An outfielder by trade, he played for the Cleveland Indians from 1943 through early 1948 then moved on to the Chicago White Sox for parts of two seasons. He retired with seven years' service and those less-than-sparkling aforementioned statistics.

But for one day, Pat Seerey was unstoppable: in an eleven-inning game on July 18, 1948, Seerey cracked four home runs, joining only nine other players to accomplish that feat in the twentieth century. If fans took this performance as a sign of great things to come, they would be disappointed. Seerey hit only 15 other home runs the entire season, 86 for his whole career.

One summer day, Pat's bat showed signs of life—but life that would quickly fade away. Jesus' parable of the seeds comes to mind: When the "farmer" sows the Word of God, some people, "like seed sown on rocky places, hear the word and at once receive it with joy. But since they have no root, they last only a short time. When trouble or persecution comes because of the word, they quickly fall away" (Mark 4:16–17). Happily, there are others, "like seed sown on good soil, [who] hear the word, accept it, and produce a crop—some thirty, some sixty, some a hundred times what was sown" (Mark 4:20).

Which kind of person are you?

> "As for everyone who comes to me and hears my words and puts them into practice, I will show you what they are like. They are like a man building a house, who dug down deep and laid the foundation on rock. When a flood came, the torrent struck that house but could not shake it, because it was well built."
>
> LUKE 6:47–48

Look over the bronze plaques in the Baseball Hall of Fame and you'll see something unusual about Charles Hafey's: he's one of very few players depicted wearing glasses.

Hafey, whose nickname was "Chick," played for the St. Louis Cardinals from 1924 to 1931 and the Cincinnati Reds from 1932 to 1937. He was the first major league

**IN-SIGHT**

outfielder to wear glasses, and in 1931 he became the first batting champion in spectacles. He hit .349 that year while compiling a league-best on-base percentage of .404.

For the man with the assisted vision, those numbers were no flukes. Hafey hit over .300 in nine of his thirteen major league seasons, finishing with a .317 career batting average. His batting and slugging figures both rank in baseball's all-time Top 100.

Chick Hafey's glasses weren't an embarrassment or a sign of weakness. Without a doubt, they gave him the clarity he needed to hit the ball—and to put up the numbers that earned his ticket to Cooperstown. In the same way, we as Christians need clarity to achieve success in our own lives. The book of James talks about a spiritual vision booster that promises amazing results: "If any of you lacks wisdom, you should ask God, who gives generously to all without finding fault, and it will be given to you" (James 1:5).

We need all the help we can get to fight off the curveballs—and avoid the beanballs—of this life. Don't be afraid to ask God for the clarity you need.

*Teach us to number our days, that*
*we may gain a heart of wisdom.*
PSALM 90:12

Ron Hunt earned his baseball fame painfully.

Primarily a second baseman, Hunt spent twelve years in the major leagues, playing with the New York Mets, Los Angeles Dodgers, San Francisco Giants, Montreal Expos, and St. Louis Cardinals between 1963 and 1974. Though he was twice selected an All-Star (in 1964 and 1966), his career numbers were nothing special: a .273 batting average, 370 runs batted in, and 39 home runs.

## WEARING A TARGET

But the St. Louis native excelled in one particular category: seven times in his dozen seasons, Hunt led the National League in being hit by pitches. In both 1968 and '69, with the Giants, he was plunked 25 times then upped his total to 26 the following season. In 1971, as an Expo, he set a modern major league record by taking *50* shots. The next three years saw league-leading totals of 26, 24, and 16, respectively, before Hunt retired from the game.

As the National League's "beanbag" for seven straight seasons, Ron Hunt must have felt like he was wearing a target on his back. If you believe in Jesus, you're wearing a bull's-eye, too.

The apostle Paul told the Christians in Ephesus that the devil has "schemes" against us—and we're in the crosshairs of his evil sights. The good news is that we have a defense: "Take up the shield of faith, with which you can extinguish all the flaming arrows of the evil one" (Ephesians 6:16).

That shield—your confidence in God—is just one part of a whole suit of armor Paul describes in Ephesians 6:11–18. Are you wearing yours today?

*Above all else, guard your heart,*
*for everything you do flows from it.*
PROVERBS 4:23

In terms of baseball notoriety, Pete Fox was either blessed or cursed to have a career coinciding with Jimmie Foxx's.

Pete, an outfielder with both the Detroit Tigers and Boston Red Sox, debuted in 1933, the ninth season of future Hall of Famer Jimmie Foxx. Both men would play into 1945 before retiring.

**SINGLE X**

In his twenty-year career, Jimmie recorded an overall batting average of .325 with 534 home runs and 1,922 runs batted in. Over thirteen years, Pete had five seasons in which he hit over .300—including a career-best .331 with the Tigers in 1937. He batted .385 in Detroit's 1935 World Series championship and left the game with a lifetime average of .298. His home run and RBI totals were 65 and 694, respectively.

Though Pete's numbers would never stack up to superstar Jimmie's, he did gain a certain repute from his similar last name. Fans began calling Pete "Single X" to differentiate him from Jimmie—the "Double X."

Among Jesus' disciples were two men with the same name: Judas. One named Judas Iscariot is well known as the betrayer of Jesus. The other Judas is mentioned a handful of times and heard from just once, in John 14:22: "Then Judas (not Judas Iscariot) said. . . ."

The point is not what Judas said that day, but simply the fact that he could be distinguished from the *other* Judas—the bad guy of the Gospel story.

What sets you apart from the world you live in? If there's no clear distinction—a "Single X/Double X" or "not Judas Iscariot" answer—then you have an important job ahead of you today.

*Live such good lives among the pagans that, though they accuse you of doing wrong, they may see your good deeds and glorify God on the day he visits us.*
1 PETER 2:12

Hitting was Ralph Kiner's forte. Fielding was clearly secondary.

For seven straight years, beginning with his 1946 rookie season, Kiner led the National League in home runs. The Pittsburgh outfielder knocked 23 dingers as a freshman then slammed 51 the following year. Totals of 40, 54, 47, 42, and 37 followed, until he was finally unseated as home run king by Milwaukee's Eddie Mathews in 1953.

## SPECIFIC CONTRIBUTIONS

Along the way, Kiner posted league-leading figures in runs scored (124 in 1951), runs batted in (127 in 1949), bases on balls (117, 137, and 110 in 1949, '51, and '52), on-base percentage (.452 in 1951), and slugging average (.639, .658, and .627 in 1947, '49, and '51). All that hitting ultimately led Ralph Kiner to baseball's Hall of Fame in 1975.

On defense, Kiner was less imposing, with a bit of a bad rap for his glove and arm in left field. St. Louis Cardinal and fellow Hall of Famer Enos Slaughter claimed he could score against Kiner on balls hit only 30 feet behind third base.

But that was all right—Kiner was expected to contribute in his area of strength. In the Christian life, we call those areas of strength "gifts," given by God Himself.

If you prefer to serve God by delivering meals to the elderly than by teaching a Sunday school class, that's all right. Or if you're happier mowing grass at the church than going on a missions trip, it's all good in God's eyes: "Just as each of us has one body with many members, and these members do not all have the same function, so in Christ we, though many, form one body, and each member belongs to all the others" (Romans 12:4–5).

Where do you excel? That's probably the place God wants you to serve today.

*There are different kinds of gifts, but the same Spirit distributes them.*
*There are different kinds of service, but the same Lord.*
1 CORINTHIANS 12:4–5

In the late 1990s, baseball's version of Dr. Jekyll and Mr. Hyde made its home in sunny south Florida.

You've heard the story—the Marlins, in just their fifth year of existence, parlayed a wild card playoff berth into the 1997 World Series championship. Then team leaders dumped their high-priced stars, and Florida finished the following season dead last.

**THOSE '98 MARLINS**

Key players who made Miami sing and Cleveland weep in late '97 were gone in early '98: starting pitcher Kevin Brown to San Diego; closer Robb Nen to San Francisco; first baseman Jeff Conine to Kansas City; and outfielder Moises Alou to Houston. They called it a "fire sale."

Other stars—including Bobby Bonilla, Gary Sheffield, and Charles Johnson—would depart the Marlins just weeks into the new campaign. Florida manager Jim Leyland found himself in a no-win situation—or, more accurately, a 54-win situation. With a hefty 108 losses, the Marlins had the worst record in baseball that year.

Florida had been to the mountaintop, only to slide headlong into the valley below. That's a danger for us as Christians, too, if we allow the world to distract us from following God wholeheartedly. In the book of Revelation, Jesus praised the Ephesian Christians for their hard work and perseverance, but He chided them for having "forsaken the love you had at first" (Revelation 2:4). To return to God's good graces, Jesus told them to "consider how far you have fallen! Repent and do the things you did at first" (Revelation 2:5).

If you've gotten off your game, all is not lost. Just as the Marlins returned to the top in 2003, you can return to God. He'll always restore those who repent.

*Return to the LORD your God, for he is gracious and compassionate, slow to anger and abounding in love.*
JOEL 2:13

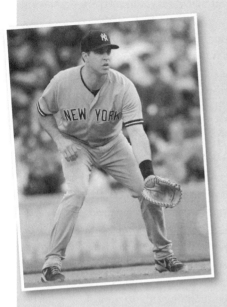

# MARK TEIXEIRA

### *Nickname:* Tex

**Quote:** "Our deeds don't make us righteous. Our deeds don't make us worthy to be in God's presence or to be in His kingdom. God's righteousness is given to us, and His grace is given to us as a gift."

## AWARDS AND HONORS

- All-Star 2005, 2009
- Gold Glove 2005, 2006, 2009, 2010, 2012
- Silver Slugger 2004, 2005, 2009

## MINISTRIES

- Scholarship programs
- Harlem RBI and DREAM charter school, providing sports, educational, and enrichment opportunities for inner-city youth

With the American League's expansion from eight to ten teams, Southern California hoped to experience a little baseball heaven.

For its first sixty years, the junior circuit played primarily in the east—with Milwaukee, St. Louis, and Kansas City as it westernmost outposts. But in 1961, when Angels touched down in Los Angeles, the American League was truly continental in scope.

**HALOS**

Led by outfielder Albie Pearson, whose .420 on-base percentage was fourth in the league, and pitcher Ken McBride, whose 180 strikeouts were the American League's fifth best, the Angels finished 70–91, in eighth place, 38½ games behind pennant-winning New York. Still, fans flocked to see the team.

In 2002, reconstituted as the Anaheim Angels, they would nab their first World Series title, downing the San Francisco Giants in seven games. Manager Mike Scioscia's team, featuring Troy Percival, Bengie Molina, David Eckstein, and Tim Salmon, finally gave Angels fans the taste of baseball heaven they craved.

Angels and heaven just go together, don't they? Well, not always.

Describing the kind of false teacher who "preaches a Jesus other than the Jesus we preached" (2 Corinthians 11:4), the apostle Paul compared these "deceitful workers, masquerading as apostles of Christ" to Satan himself, who "masquerades as an angel of light" (2 Corinthians 11:13–14).

There may be ideas, teachings, and attitudes in the "Christian" world that aren't Christian at all—and Satan can use them to pull people away from the true faith. Our job is to know the Bible well enough to determine what's worth following—and what we need to avoid like an inning-ending double play.

Not every halo hints of heaven.

*But even if we or an angel from heaven should preach a gospel other than the one we preached to you, let them be under God's curse!*
GALATIANS 1:8

August Joseph Williams' career overlapped briefly with that of the great Babe Ruth. But that was about Gus' only brush with baseball immortality.

The Omaha, Nebraska, native broke into the major leagues in 1911

**GUS WILLIAMS**

as a twenty-two-year-old rookie with the St. Louis Browns. He played seven games in left field, recording a less-than-stellar fielding average of .867, and batted in nine games, averaging .269 over 26 at bats.

In succeeding seasons, Williams moved to right field, where he would appear in 381 games over the next four years. His five-year major league career featured a .939 fielding average and a .263 batting average with 12 lifetime home runs in 410 at bats. Williams played each of his five years with the Browns, a perennial second-division team. "Mundane" well describes his career.

So why make August Joseph Williams the focus of today's reading? Simply to comment on his nickname: "Gloomy Gus." Apparently, he was a sourpuss in the dugout.

Christians have no reason to feel, act, or be called "gloomy." Even in the worst circumstance, our relationship to God and our hope of heaven should keep us from sliding into an extended slump. Consider the apostles' reaction to their own arrest, imprisonment, and flogging at the hands of the high priest and the Sadducees soon after Pentecost: "The apostles left the Sanhedrin, rejoicing because they had been counted worthy of suffering disgrace for the Name" (Acts 5:41).

Life will have its ups and downs—but joy, not gloom, is the defining emotion of the Christian experience.

*Though you have not seen him, you love him; and even though you do not see him now, you believe in him and are filled with an inexpressible and glorious joy, for you are receiving the end result of your faith, the salvation of your souls.*
1 PETER 1:8–9

Baseball abounds with statistics, some measuring success and others failure. "Games behind" leans toward the latter.

In the standings, the GB column lets a fan judge the relative distance between the leader and other teams in a division. To calculate, subtract the follower's wins from the leader's wins; then subtract the leader's losses from the

**GAMES BEHIND**

follower's losses. Add the differences and divide by two for "games behind." By season's end, each team except the division champion will have a GB total, showing just how close it came to success. For many, often expansion clubs, it wasn't close at all.

Consider Tampa Bay, debuting in the American League East in 1998 with baseball's second-worst record (63–99). When the New York Yankees won a record 114 games, the Devil Rays ended up 51 games behind. It was even worse for the New York Mets in 1962: the newbies of the National League went 40–120 as the San Francisco Giants finished 103–62, and the GB column showed 60½. But the all-time futility record belongs to the 1899 Cleveland Spiders, playing their final season in the National League. They were truly awful at 20–134, a whopping 85½ games behind the Brooklyn Bridegrooms.

But the wide gaps between those first- and last-place teams are nothing compared to the distance between human beings and God. The apostle Paul told how people are "separate from Christ . . . without hope and without God in the world" (Ephesians 2:12). As is always the case with God, though, there's good news, too: through Jesus' blood, Paul continued, "you who once were far away have been brought near" (Ephesians 2:13).

When you're in Christ, the wide gap is no longer between you and God but between you and your sins.

*As far as the east is from the west, so far*
*has he removed our transgressions from us.*
PSALM 103:12

Mel Ott's achievements as a player earned him a ticket to Cooperstown. One bad day as a manager earned him a spot in the history books.

The slugging outfielder spent his entire twenty-two-year playing career

**BLAZING A TRAIL**

with the New York Giants. As a rookie in 1926, Ott was hot, posting a .383 average in 60 at bats. His sophomore season was less impressive; his batting average dropped more than a hundred points to .282. Ott did, however, hit the first home run of his major league career—and over the next two decades would slam 510 more to earn a spot on baseball's all-time Top 20 list.

From 1942 to '47, the man from Gretna, Louisiana, pulled double duty as New York's player-manager then finished his Giant service in 1948 by acting solely as manager. His career as a field commander was less than sparkling, leading the Giants to just three winning seasons and a best finish of third place his first season. It was in managing, though, that Ott blazed a trail to the record books in a dubious fashion. On June 9, 1946, he became the first major league manager ever ejected from both games of a doubleheader.

Heckling umpires is a time-honored tradition of managers, but too much temper can lead to the old heave-ho. In baseball, the long-term consequences are relatively limited. In our lives, though, temper can create all sorts of problems in our personal, business, and church relationships. That's why the world's wisest man, King Solomon, wrote, "Better a patient person than a warrior, one with self-control than one who takes a city" (Proverbs 16:32).

Next time you're angry, think of Mel Ott's "legacy"—and blaze your own trail to self-control.

> *My dear brothers and sisters, take note of this: Everyone should be quick to listen, slow to speak, and slow to become angry.*
> JAMES 1:19

"The Mechanical Man" was what they called Charlie Gehringer, and it was meant as a compliment.

In a nineteen-year career played entirely with the Detroit Tigers, the second baseman was a model of consistency. From 1928 to 1930, again in 1933 and '34, and once more in 1936, Gehringer led the American League in **MR. CONSISTENCY**
games played, with 154 or 155 each season. For thirteen of the fourteen years in the middle of his career, he batted over .300—including a league-leading .371 in 1937—and the one year he missed he hit .298. On defense, Gehringer turned in league-high fielding percentages in 1929, '30, '35, '36, '37, '39, and '41. And for six straight years, from 1933 through 1938, the Mechanical Man was selected to the All-Star team.

A Tiger teammate once said of Gehringer, "You wind him up on Opening Day and forget about him." That's the thing with mechanical men—they may not be flashy or draw attention to themselves, but they get the job done. Persistence, hard work, and consistency win in the long run, whether for baseball players or for us as Christians.

So what does a "Mechanical (Christian) Man," a "Mr. (Spiritual) Consistency" look like? Maybe something like the apostle Paul described in Philippians 1:27: "Whatever happens, conduct yourself in a manner worthy of the gospel of Christ." In good times or bad, whether it's easy or hard, that means love for neighbors, honesty in business, purity in relationships, faithfulness in service.

Ultimately, there's the reward of God's "Well done. . . . Come and share your master's happiness!" (Matthew 25:23).

*Who is wise and understanding among you? Let them show it by their good life, by deeds done in the humility that comes from wisdom.*
JAMES 3:13

Modern bull pens are filled with specialists—long relievers, short relievers, setup men, and closers—and it's relatively rare today for starting pitchers to finish their own games.

**COMPLETE GAMES**

In the major leagues' early years, though, a starter was more apt to see a game from the first pitch to the last. The great Cy Young holds the career record for complete games (a record that will never be broken) with 749. Rounding out the top five—Pud Galvin with 639, Tim Keefe with 554, and Walter Johnson and Kid Nichols, each with 531—are pitchers who were all, like Young, born in the nineteenth century.

During the 1942 season, Chicago White Sox right-hander Ted Lyons wrote himself into the history books by completing every one of the 20 games he started. Lyons, in his twentieth year with the Pale Hose, went 14–6 with a league-leading 2.10 earned run average.

All six pitchers mentioned above are now in the Hall of Fame, as the power to finish generates respect. That's a power God shows to His own, according to Philippians 1:4–6, where the apostle Paul writes, "I always pray with joy . . . being confident of this, that he who began a good work in you will carry it on to completion until the day of Christ Jesus."

When you accept Christ, God makes a commitment to see you through to heaven—whatever temptations, fears, struggles, and failures you may experience along the way. Though you're expected to obey God's various commands, you should be encouraged to know that your ultimate success is in His very capable hands. The "complete game" is God's task, not yours.

*I know whom I have believed, and am convinced that he is able to guard what I have entrusted to him until that day.*
2 TIMOTHY 1:12

Skim through the all-time roster of more than sixteen thousand players, and you can have some fun with the names of certain major leaguers. How about creating an "All Body Team"?

Here's the lineup:

- Dave Brain, infielder/outfielder (White Sox, Cardinals, Pirates, Braves, Reds, and Giants, 1901–08)
- Ed Head, pitcher (Brooklyn, 1940–46)
- Elroy Face, pitcher (Pirates, Tigers, and Expos, 1953–69)
- Jim Ray Hart, third baseman and outfielder (Giants and Yankees, 1963–74)
- Rich Hand, pitcher (Indians, Rangers, and Angels, 1970–73)
- Rollie Fingers, pitcher (A's, Padres, and Brewers, 1968–85)
- Greg Legg, infielder (Phillies, 1986–87)
- Barry Foote, catcher (Expos, Phillies, Cubs, and Yankees, 1973–1982).

Heads, arms, hands, and legs combine to form a body, much as pitchers, catchers, infielders, and outfielders come together to create a baseball team. Each one is equally important and completely dependent on the others—as is the case with Christians, who collectively make up the "body of Christ."

For those of us who might envy the gifts, abilities, and position of others, the apostle Paul painted an amusing word picture. Urging Christians to appreciate whatever role they play, he wrote, "If the whole body were an eye, where would the sense of hearing be? If the whole body were an ear, where would the sense of smell be? But in fact God has placed the parts in the body, every one of them, just as he wanted them to be" (1 Corinthians 12:17–18).

Whether you're a Head, a Hand, or a Foote, you're an indispensable part of the family of God. Find your job and do it well!

*For we are members of his body.*
EPHESIANS 5:30

Decades of major league play occurred before a regular catcher had a perfect season.

When the National League asserted its dominance in 1893 and settled

**CATCHING PERFECTION**

the distance between the pitcher's mound and home plate at 60 feet, 6 inches, the modern era of Major League Baseball began. It would be another fifty-three years before Buddy Rosar turned in the first errorless campaign for a backstop.

Rosar caught a career-high 121 games for the Philadelphia Athletics in 1946, recording a flawless fielding average of 1.000 for the season. His sparkling play notwithstanding, the A's finished in the American League cellar, 55 games behind first-place Boston.

Four times in thirteen years of play, Rosar led the league in fielding average, finishing with a career figure of .992, better than Hall of Fame catchers Johnny Bench (.990), Yogi Berra (.989), and Carlton Fisk and Roy Campanella (both .988). Though Berra would match his Philadelphia counterpart's single-season feat twelve years later, Rosar went down in baseball history as the first catcher to reach that level of perfection.

Jesus once commanded His followers to "Be perfect . . . as your heavenly Father is perfect" (Matthew 5:48). As if that weren't hard enough, the order follows a discourse on loving our enemies. Can you possibly do that? Only if, as the apostle Paul prayed, "out of [God's] glorious riches he may strengthen you with power through his Spirit" (Ephesians 3:16).

That's the only way you'll ever catch perfection.

> *Be perfect . . . and the God of love*
> *and peace shall be with you.*
> 2 CORINTHIANS 13:11 KJV

# MARIANO RIVERA

**_Nickname:_** Mo,
The Sandman

**Quote:** "Every time I was
going through a hard time,
somebody was there to help.
Even though I had nobody
here [in the United States], I was never alone. That made
me accept Jesus as my Savior. I knew it wasn't a coincidence. It was the
Lord putting someone there for me."

## AWARDS AND HONORS

- All-Star 1997, 1999, 2000, 2001, 2002, 2004, 2005, 2006, 2008, 2009, 2010, 2011, 2013
- American League Rolaids Relief Award 1999, 2001, 2004, 2005, 2009
- American League Babe Ruth Award 1999
- World Series MVP 1999
- American League Championship Series MVP 2001
- All-Star Game MVP 2013

## MINISTRIES

- Restoring Refugio de Esperanza Church, New Rochelle, New York
- The Mariano Rivera Foundation, serving underprivileged youth in the United States and Panama
- Plans to enter ministry after retiring from baseball

For a shining moment in 2006, Endy Chavez was the Big Apple's biggest hero.

The setting: Game 7 of the National League Championship Series

**ULTIMATE LOSS**

between New York and St. Louis. In the sixth inning, with the score tied at one, the Cardinals' Scott Rolen ripped a long fly ball to left field. Chavez tracked it down, jumped high against the wall, and robbed Rolen of a go-ahead homer. The native Venezuelan's heroics preserved the tie and later earned mention in CNN/SI.com's "2006 Games of the Year" retrospective as "one of the most memorable postseason catches ever."

Unfortunately for Chavez and his fellow Mets, the Cardinals would go on to record a 3–1 victory, as St. Louis advanced to the World Series against the American League champion Detroit Tigers. The outfielder's sparkling achievement wasn't enough to stave off ultimate loss.

That "ultimate loss" idea has a chilling tone in Jesus' description of people trying to use personal accomplishments as their ticket to heaven. "Many will say to me on that day, 'Lord, Lord, did we not prophesy in your name and in your name drive out demons and in your name perform many miracles?' Then I will tell them plainly, 'I never knew you. Away from me, you evildoers!' " (Matthew 7:22–23). Jesus' name, powerful as it may be, is no magic charm: "Not everyone who says to me, 'Lord, Lord,' will enter the kingdom of heaven," He said (Matthew 7:21a). Who will then? "Only the one who does the will of my Father who is in heaven" (Matthew 7:21b).

Is it worth a few minutes today to make sure you're doing God's will?

*Therefore, my brothers and sisters, make every effort to confirm your calling and election.*

2 Peter 1:10

Kenesaw Mountain Landis started his career in law. He ended up a baseball Hall of Famer—and he never stepped inside the baselines.

Born in Ohio and named after a Civil War battlefield (his father had been wounded there), Landis became a judge in 1905. Sixteen years later he was named the first commissioner of Major League Baseball.

**IMMEDIATE HONOR**

Team owners liked Landis' plainspoken, no-nonsense style and gave him wide power to rule the game rocked by the 1919 "Black Sox" gambling scandal. Though the Chicago players were acquitted at trial, the new commissioner banned them for life anyway. Players came to fear Landis, who himself seemed fearless: he suspended Babe Ruth for a month in 1922 (for taking part in a barnstorming tour) and forced Ban Johnson, the founder and president of the American League, from his position in 1927.

In time, owners came to regret the powers they'd given the commissioner—and players found, to their surprise, that Landis often took their side in labor disputes. Loved or hated, Kenesaw Mountain Landis was a dominant figure in the game of baseball. Upon his death in 1944, he was immediately voted into the Hall of Fame.

Christians can look forward to an immediate honor of a greater sort: when we die, we're promoted not to an earthly museum but to the perfection of heaven. "We are confident, I say," wrote the apostle Paul, "and would prefer to be away from the body and at home with the Lord" (2 Corinthians 5:8).

Sure, honors in this life are nice. But being with Jesus, Paul said, "is better by far" (Philippians 1:23).

*Then [the dying criminal] said, "Jesus, remember me*
*when you come into your kingdom." Jesus answered him,*
*"Truly I tell you, today you will be with me in paradise."*
LUKE 23:42–43

Joe Sewell got a big break in the fall of 1920. The first-year pro, toiling in Class A ball in Louisiana, earned every player's dream when he was called up to the big leagues.

**BIG SHOES**

Not quite twenty-two years old, Sewell hit .329 over the final three weeks of the season, helping the Cleveland Indians clinch their first American League pennant and World Series championship. Sewell's performance is all the more remarkable considering the situation he walked into: Indians manager Tris Speaker plugged Sewell into the position of beloved shortstop Ray Chapman, who had been killed by a pitch in August.

As things turned out, Sewell was no September flash in the pan. The Alabama native played a total of thirteen full seasons in the majors, compiling a lifetime batting average of .312, including a personal best .353 in 1923. He was nearly impossible to strike out, as he fanned only four times in 155 games in 1925; in his career, over a span of 7,132 plate appearances, Sewell struck out only 113 times. In 1977 he would be elected to the Hall of Fame.

Sewell's life has similarities to that of the biblical Joshua. Following the towering figure of Moses, Joshua took over the leadership of Israel and immediately made his own mark. Then, in years following, the son of Nun continued to impress. A focus on fundamentals was key: "Be strong and very courageous. Be careful to obey all the law my servant Moses gave you; do not turn from it to the right or to the left, that you may be successful wherever you go. Keep this Book of the Law always on your lips; meditate on it day and night, so that you may be careful to do everything written in it" (Joshua 1:7–8).

Sometime you'll probably have to step into a difficult situation. Follow Joe's and Joshua's lead in filling those big shoes.

> *"As I was with Moses, so I will be with you;*
> *I will never leave you nor forsake you."*
> JOSHUA 1:5

Ever heard of Old Judge, Gypsy Queen, or Turkey Red? They're not player nicknames, but tobacco brands that produced the earliest baseball trading cards.

In 1887 the cigarette maker Allen & Ginter offered one of the first sports card **BASEBALL CARDS** sets with future Hall of Famers Cap Anson (member of the 3,000 hit club, lifetime average of .332) and Charles Comiskey (owner of the Chicago White Sox from 1900 to 1931) among the ten baseball figures featured. The set included other sports, too, highlighting notable figures like boxer Jack Dempsey and shooter Annie Oakley.

Baseball cards, though, had the staying power, and production shifted to candy and gum makers by the 1930s. Under the Topps brand, the card business boomed in the early 1950s. This "golden era" generated one of the most sought-after of all baseball collectibles, the 1952 Mickey Mantle rookie card, which reportedly sold for $275,000 in 2001.

While early cards carried scant player information on the reverse, Topps used that space for a brief biography and personal statistics. Collectors could learn the birth date, height, weight, and other data on a given player, as well as his on-the-field numbers—games played, at bats or innings pitched, base hits obtained or strikeouts thrown, and so on. Over the years, baseball cards summarized the evolving careers of tens of thousands of major leaguers.

What if there were "baseball cards" for us as Christians? What kind of statistics might they include?

The list of the "fruit of the Spirit" in Galatians 5:22–23 provides nine important categories: love, joy, peace, forbearance, kindness, goodness, faithfulness, gentleness, and self-control.

How are you doing in those areas? More importantly, would succeeding years' cards show improvement in each column?

*If you possess these qualities in increasing measure,*
*they will keep you from being ineffective and unproductive*
*in your knowledge of our Lord Jesus Christ.*
2 PETER 1:8

Call it the "dark side" of America's Pastime.

When a baseball becomes a tool of intimidation, trouble often follows. Countless stare downs, fistfights, and melees have occurred in response to pitches that came close to—or collided with—batters.

## BRUSHBACKS AND BEANBALLS

Brushbacks are throws intended to move a hitter away from the plate. "It's just plain foolishness to let a batter dig in on you," said right-hander Bobo Newsom (who played from 1929 to 1953), defending the high, tight pitch. "You've got to let those fellows hit the dirt, or they'll take the food right out of your mouth."

Beanballs, meanwhile, actually connect with the batter's head (the "bean" in old-time terminology)—sometimes with serious result. In 1937, for example, Detroit catcher Mickey Cochrane's skull was fractured when he was beaned by the Yankees' Bump Hadley. Hadley's missile was seen as retaliation for a home run Cochrane had hit earlier.

The retaliatory pitch is a not-so-secret aspect of the game. In 1976 Baltimore's Jim Palmer, a future Hall of Famer who hit only thirty-eight batters in 3,948 career innings, plunked New York's Mickey Rivers in the back after Yankee pitcher Dock Ellis beaned the O's Reggie Jackson. "Our best hitter gets hit in the face, and who knows how long he's going to be out?" Palmer said. "You've got to do something to protect your hitters."

Those baseball-style paybacks appeal to our competitive human nature. But, according to the apostle Peter, they're not the biblical way: "Do not repay evil with evil or insult with insult. On the contrary, repay evil with blessing, because to this you were called so that you may inherit a blessing" (1 Peter 3:9).

Self-control is a fruit of God's Spirit inside you (see Galatians 5:22–23). Today, will you show retaliation or restraint?

*Do not say, "I'll pay you back for this wrong!"*
*Wait for the LORD, and he will avenge you.*
PROVERBS 20:22

A little support goes a long way for a pitcher. Just ask Bill Lee.

"Big Bill," a right-hander known for his high leg kick, led the Chicago Cubs to the 1938 pennant by posting league-leading statistics in wins (22), winning percentage (.710), and earned run average (2.66). He added a personal-best 37 starts, 291 innings pitched, and 121 strikeouts that season as well, helping his

**LACK OF SUPPORT**

Cubs to an 89–63 finish, two games ahead of the second-place Pittsburgh Pirates.

The offensive support Lee had enjoyed throughout the season, though, evaporated in the World Series as Cub hitters managed only a single run during his twelve innings on the mound. Even the defense failed him, as Chicago fielders committed a pair of crucial errors. Those Cub miscues, occurring at a critical time, contributed to a four-game series sweep by the New York Yankees.

In a far graver situation, Jesus saw His support disappear when, at the moment of His arrest, "all the disciples deserted him and fled" (Matthew 26:56). Shortly afterward, Jesus' prophecy about Peter came true: "Before the rooster crows today, you will deny three times that you know me" (Luke 22:34). Those crushing failures seemed to lead to the worst defeat imaginable—Jesus' death on the cross.

But if you're at all familiar with the life of Jesus, you know that He rose again—then forgave and restored the men who had failed Him so miserably. Even better, He's ready to forgive and restore *you* when you fail Him.

*If we confess our sins, he is faithful and just and will*
*forgive us our sins and purify us from all unrighteousness.*
1 JOHN 1:9

It seems appropriate that "America's Pastime" would have deep connections to US presidents.

William Howard Taft started the tradition of presidents throwing out a

**FAMOUS NAMES**

ceremonial first pitch. During World War II, Franklin D. Roosevelt urged the major leagues to continue playing to maintain America's morale. George W. Bush actually ran a major league team, the Texas Rangers, before he became president.

No president has ever played Major League Baseball, but several big-leaguers have borne presidential names. There was George Washington, patrolling the outfield for the White Sox in 1935 and '36, and three different Jeffersons, most recently Reggie, playing for the Reds, Indians, Mariners, and Red Sox between 1991 and 1999. A John Kennedy played for the Phillies in 1957, and another one for six teams between 1962 and 1974. Two have sported the name Lincoln, six Nixon, more than a dozen each for Ford and Carter, plus one Reagan, two Clintons, and five Bushes.

Some names stand out as "famous," but none will ever compare with that of Jesus Christ. The Son of God, who left the perfection of heaven to be born in a Judean barn, has been exalted "to the highest place" with a name "that is above every name, that at the name of Jesus, every knee should bow, in heaven and on earth and under the earth, and every tongue acknowledge that Jesus Christ is Lord, to the glory of God the Father" (Philippians 2:9–11).

Have you spoken that name today?

*"You will conceive and give birth to a son, and you are to call him Jesus. He will be great and will be called the Son of the Most High."*
LUKE 1:31–32

Fred "Dixie" Walker was on a roll, having earned five straight All-Star nods with the Brooklyn Dodgers. Then he was gone, traded to the Pittsburgh Pirates.

So what was that all about?

## THE PEOPLE'S CHERCE—AH, CHOICE

It wasn't his popularity with the fans—they loved the outfielder called "The People's Cherce." It wasn't his hitting—his .306 average in 1947, Walker's last year with Brooklyn, was his fifth straight .300-plus campaign. Three years before, he'd led the league with a healthy .357 average.

What sent Dixie Walker packing was his attitude—specifically, his attitude toward teammate Jackie Robinson, the first black player in the modern major leagues. Dixie, a son of the Old South, had stated he wouldn't play on the same team as the 1947 Rookie of the Year. Dodgers' general manager Branch Rickey, who had personally selected Robinson as the player to break baseball's "color line," took Walker at his word—and shipped his proud star off to the Steel City. (This story was highlighted in the brilliant 2013 movie, *42*, about Jackie Robinson integrating Major League Baseball.)

When it comes to pride, the Bible is clear: Don't go there. "Pride goes before destruction, a haughty spirit before a fall," was Solomon's warning in Proverbs 16:18. Proverbs 11:2 provides both negative and positive reinforcement: "When pride comes, then comes disgrace, but with humility comes wisdom."

If you're ever tempted to "think of yourself more highly than you ought" (Romans 12:3), think of Dixie Walker. Don't make a "cherce" you may regret.

*For everything in the world—the lust of the flesh, the lust of the eyes, and the pride of life—comes not from the Father but from the world.*
1 JOHN 2:16

Records are kept for almost every conceivable aspect of baseball—including time off before the World Series.

The Colorado Rockies enjoyed eight full days—a major league record—to rest and prepare for the 2007 World Series. It would seem that Colorado needed the rest after the Rockies' amazing late-season surge to reach their first-ever Fall Classic: they won 13 of their final 14 regular season games to clinch the National League wild card then swept the Chicago Cubs and Arizona Diamondbacks in the playoffs. All told, Colorado won 21 of its last 22 games to reach the World Series.

**TIME OFF**

When Boston swept the Rockies in the Fall Classic, some observers speculated that *too much* time off may have hurt Colorado. But, generally speaking, nobody questions the value of rest.

The idea of rest actually has biblical roots, going as far back as the seventh day of creation. And God reemphasized the idea when He gave the Law to Moses: "Six days do your work, but on the seventh day do not work, so that your ox and your donkey may rest and the slave born in your household, and the foreigner living among you may be refreshed" (Exodus 23:12).

For the ancient Jews, this "Sabbath day" was a religious duty—but one with a practical benefit. Even Jesus, who dismissed the restrictive Sabbath rules of the scribes and Pharisees, encouraged His disciples to take time off for rest.

Should we do any less?

*The apostles gathered around Jesus and reported to him all they had done and taught. Then, because so many people were coming and going that they did not even have a chance to eat, he said to them, "Come with me by yourselves to a quiet place and get some rest."*

MARK 6:30–31

"Base stealing threat" was not emphasized in Vic Power's scouting reports.

The native Puerto Rican played twelve major league seasons with the Philadelphia and Kansas City Athletics, the Cleveland Indians, the Minnesota Twins, the Los Angeles and California Angels, and the Philadelphia Phillies. In those dozen years, covering 1954 to '65, Power stole a total of 45 bases, an average of just three or four a year.

**SEIZE THE OPPORTUNITY**

A lifetime .284 hitter who played primarily at first base, Power swiped the most bases during 1959 and '60, a pair of All-Star seasons with the Indians. He stole nine in each of those years, though he was also caught a total of eighteen times.

In 1958 when Power split his season between Kansas City and Cleveland, he stole his usual three bases—but, interestingly, two of those steals were of home plate. Even more remarkably, they occurred in the same game, on August 14 for the Indians against the Detroit Tigers.

For a guy who rarely ventured onto the base paths, swiping home twice in one game was a great example of seizing an opportunity. The apostle Paul would likely have approved.

In two of his letters, Paul urged believers to take advantage of every chance to be light in a dark world. "Be very careful, then, how you live— not as unwise but as wise, making the most of every opportunity, because the days are evil," is the message of Ephesians 5:15–16. Colossians 4:5 reads, "Be wise in the way you act toward outsiders; make the most of every opportunity."

We have a chance to show Jesus Christ to the world every day. Will you seize those opportunities?

*Whoever claims to live in [God] must live as Jesus did.*
1 JOHN 2:6

Mark Fidrych was a bit different. You might expect that from a man nicknamed for a *Sesame Street* character.

A minor league coach called Fidrych "Bird" because the 6-foot, 3-inch,

**A LITTLE ODD**

175-pound right-hander reminded him of the tall, yellow-feathered Muppet named Big Bird. Beyond his appearance, Fidrych stood out for goofy antics on the mound—including talking to the baseball. Whatever he said to the horsehide must have worked.

The Massachusetts native arrived in the majors with Detroit in 1976. Getting his first start on May 15, Fidrych retired the first fourteen Cleveland batters he faced, giving up only two hits in a 2–1 victory. Though he lost his next start, he allowed only two runs—before notching eight straight wins, including a couple of eleven-inning complete games. By season's end, he was 19–9 with a 2.34 earned run average and 24 complete games, both American League bests. "The Bird" also started the All-Star game and won the Rookie of the Year award. The case can be made that during America's bicentennial in 1976, Fidrych was perhaps the most famous and popular athlete in the country.

Then it all went *poof*. A knee injury the next spring derailed his promising career, but Fidrych is still remembered for that one remarkable season—and for being a little odd.

"Odd" is how the world sees us as Christians, too—or worse, even as fools. Why? Because the idea of a suffering savior, hanging on a cross, doesn't really compute with human reason. "Jews demand signs and Greeks look for wisdom," the apostle Paul wrote, "but we preach Christ crucified: a stumbling block to Jews and foolishness to Gentiles." But, Paul adds, "to those whom God has called, both Jews and Greeks, Christ the power of God and the wisdom of God" (1 Corinthians 1:22–24).

So who cares if we're a little odd?

*The foolishness of God is wiser than human wisdom,*
*and the weakness of God is stronger than human strength.*

1 CORINTHIANS 1:25

Young ballplayers want to break into the majors with a bang. Old-timers hope to retire on a high note. Richie Ashburn did both.

In 1948, as a rookie center fielder with the Phillies, Ashburn batted a sparkling .333, slapping 154 hits in 117 games. He led the National League with 32 stolen bases, earned a spot on the All-Star team, and just missed the Rookie of the Year award, won by Boston Braves shortstop Alvin Dark.

## STRONG FINISH

The fabulous freshman was no fluke. Ashburn would play a total of fifteen years in the majors, batting over .300 nine times. His .338 average in 1955 and his .350 mark in 1958 were both league leading, as were his hit totals in 1951, '53, and '58 (221, 205, and 215, respectively). Four times Ashburn topped the league in on-base percentage, twice in triples, and seven times in games played.

In his final season, 1962, Ashburn earned his fifth All-Star berth. On an expansion Mets team that went 40–120, he batted .306, joining a select group of players who hit over .300 in both their first and last seasons.

That kind of strong finish was on the apostle Paul's mind as he wrote from prison to his protégé, Timothy. In what appears to be the great missionary's final letter, he said, "I have fought the good fight, I have finished the race, I have kept the faith" (2 Timothy 4:7). Though execution awaited him, Paul anticipated "the crown of righteousness, which the Lord, the righteous Judge, will award to me on that day—and not only to me, but also to all who have longed for his appearing" (2 Timothy 4:8).

Want to finish this life on a high note? Always be ready for Jesus' return.

*Blessed is the one who perseveres under trial because,*
*having stood the test, that person will receive the crown*
*of life that the Lord has promised to those who love him.*
JAMES 1:12

# INDEX OF NAMES

# M

# N

Navin, Frank—49
Nen, Robb—181
Nettles, Graig—88
Newcombe, Don—99, 141
Newsom, Bobo—196
New York Cubans—58
New York Giants—37, 38, 41, 63, 118, 124, 141, 156, 162, 186, 189
New York Mets—16, 31, 37, 50, 64, 67, 93, 100, 104, 108, 133, 140, 150, 161, 165, 167, 178, 185, 191, 203
New York Yankees—10, 13, 21, 22, 23, 25, 26, 31, 35, 43, 45, 47, 49, 59, 64, 65, 73, 74, 79, 80, 81, 82, 88, 97, 100, 102, 110, 111, 119, 124, 130, 131, 138, 142, 147, 151, 157, 159, 165, 169, 170, 174, 183, 185, 189, 196, 197
Nichols, Kid—188
Niekro, Joe—117
Nomo, Hideo—150
Nuxhall, Joe—158

# O

Oakland A's—32, 59, 75, 98, 100, 110, 114, 137, 143, 147, 151, 173, 189
Oakley, Annie—195
O'Leary, Charley—62
Olivo, Diomedes—86
O'Neil, Paul—98
O'Rourke, Jim—62
Ortiz, David—147
Ott, Mel—186

# P

Paciorek, Jim—16
Paciorek, John—16
Paciorek, Tom—16
Paige, Satchel—62, 89, 163, 166
Palmer, Jim—175, 196
Parker, Dave—104
Pearson, Albie—122, 183
Percival, Troy—183
Perez, Tony—46
Perry, Gaylord—117
Philadelphia Athletics—24, 26, 33, 71, 76, 78, 131, 136, 152, 170, 174, 190, 201
Philadelphia Phillies—9, 15, 19, 24, 46, 66, 71, 92, 107, 109, 110, 123, 129, 130, 148, 151, 156, 161, 167, 173, 189, 198, 201, 203
Philley, Dave—9

# S

# W

# Y

# Z